W9-CFQ-391

Other books by Karen Kalliopi Papagapitos-

"Artemis Bound" (2001, a collection of international poetry by the author)

"Socorro, Daughter of the Desert" (1993, award winning children's book about a young girl who understands and communicates with the desert)

"Jose's Basket" (1991,the classic story of a young migrant boy who adapts to his nomadic life by watching his mother weave grasses from each town into a basket)

Bright Friends

The First Twenty-Five Years of Visitations Tucson, Arizona 1947-1972

Karen Kalliopi Papagapitos

Karen Kalliopi Papagapitos
June 09, 2021

For Peggy-
A friend who always watches out for her friends-
Fondly-
Karen

BALBOA. PRESS
A DIVISION OF HAY HOUSE

Balboa Press books may be ordered through booksellers or by contacting:

Balboa Press
A Division of Hay House
1663 Liberty Drive
Bloomington, IN 47403
www.balboapress.com
1 (877) 407-4847

Print information available on the last page.

ISBN: 978-1-5043-6871-1 (sc)
ISBN: 978-1-5043-6872-8 (hc)
ISBN: 978-1-5043-6927-5 (e)

Library of Congress Control Number: 2016918144

Balboa Press rev. date: 11/04/2016

Contents

Part Three

Part Four

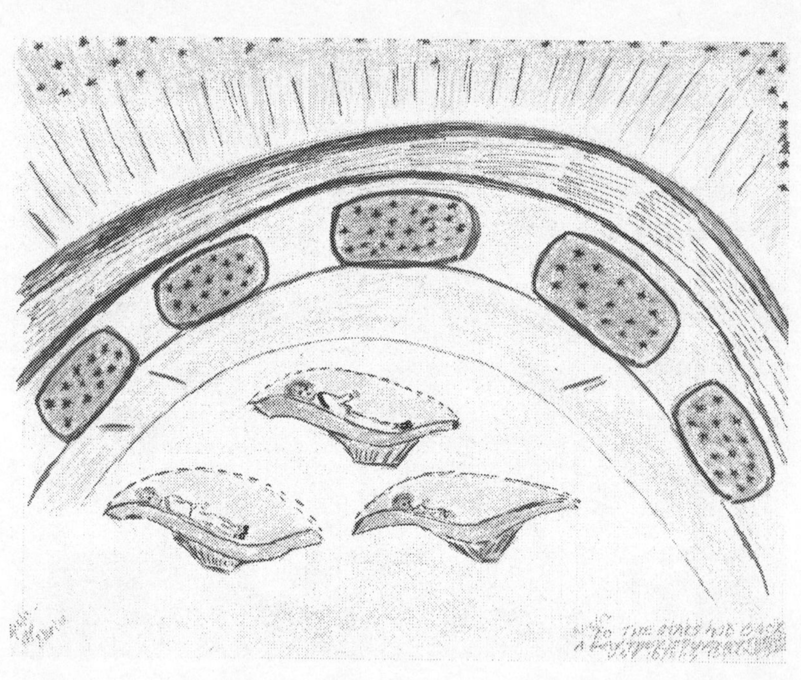

1951 "Little Boy Blue"

THE MESSENGER 1952

AFTER A HARVEST

THEY WATCHED ME SLEEP (AGES 11-19 YEARS)

'Mother Seeks Answers'

I am seven years old. My mother and I are walking toward a huge tent in the fairgrounds northwest of Tucson. The sand is hot in my sandals.

"Are we going to the circus, mommy?"

"It's not the circus, Karen"

We enter the tent. Rows of chairs lead to a stage where a man with a microphone speaks to the crowd. Another man comes up to my mother.

"Welcome, sister. Are you here for yourself or the child?"

"The child." My mother whispers.

"Is she afflicted?" The man asks.

"I don't know." My mother looks afraid.

"What's afflicted, mommy?"

"Hush Karen." Mother tells me. She looks around and seems frightened and unsure.

"Come this way." The man tries to lead us to the front of the tent.

"Let me go!" I tell him. Then to my mother again, "What's afflicted mean, mommy? Am I afflicted?"

"Quiet," she tells me and tightens her grip on my hand.

"Come, don't be afraid." The man with the smooth voice says.

My mother doesn't move; he reaches to take my hand.

"Don't touch me!" I shout and try to kick him. I miss.

"Mommy, let's go. Let's go, now!" I try to pull her toward the opening in the tent.

My mother shakes her head and focuses on the scene.

"I made a mistake; we shouldn't be here." We are both moving toward the exit now

"We can help, sister, Come back. We can help." The man with the smooth voice follows us.

"Don't be afraid; we can help the afflicted child." He points to me.

"I'm not AFFLICTED!"

My mother pulls me out of the tent. She kneels in front of me on the hot sand and embraces me.

"I'm sorry, Karen. I was wrong."

"What's afflicted, mommy. Is it bad? Am I afflicted? Don't cry, mommy. I'm alright."

We are both crying as we walk to the bus stop. The hot sun dries out tears.

"The Spaceship In My Closet: Seven Decades of Visitations"

Tucson, Arizona-1947
I was born.

Tucson, Arizona-1951

I am four years old and being carried to a beautiful ship surrounded by bright, white light in the desert. It is early morning, and the dew makes the desert fragrant. The 'being' carrying me is one of my friends; I call them my Bright Friends, because they always come in a cloud of light. Their clothes are shiney and white, with a blue stripe across the front. Some have brown hair and some have yellow/white hair.

They are beautiful, kind and funny. We learn 'games' in the little playroom on the ship. A small boy in blue overalls sits at a table with me. He wears a little cap on his head and he is not the same color as I am. He is a greyish-blue. My other friends are taller and look like my father, who is fair-haired and has very light grey eyes.

Sometimes my nose bleeds badly. I am taken to the 'doctors' on the ship. They wear all white and try to stop my nosebleeds. I show them how I can hold my head up to help stop the blood. They smile at me and I can 'feel' how much they care for me. After my nosebleed stops, I am given a sweet drink. It tastes like honey.

When they realized I was remembering, a decision on their part had to be made as to whether or not to continue my visits. A young messenger came to my room; I was allowed to be fully awake. He communicated (by thoughts and feelings…they never spoke) that they didn't know why I was remembering. 'People' usually didn't remember. They might have to stop the visits. I began to cry hysterically. He reassured me that if I didn't speak of the visits, they would continue. It would be 'better' for me if I didn't tell any adults in my life. The adults wouldn't believe me and harm might come to me. 'They' wouldn't harm me, my society would 'shun' me. The messenger communicated that I would be told I was dreaming by the adults. My Bright Friends didn't want me to think I was dreaming. The messenger communicated that this was really happening. It was real. I knew it was real. I always 'smelled the desert dew' in the night air as we approached the ship. I knew I wasn't dreaming.

Before he leaves me, he reinforces what has always been communicated by all of them: we are 'family'; we are 'related'.

For the next 21 years I am visited frequently.

During my adolescent years I am no longer with one of my Bright Friends as I travel to and from visits. The visits are less personal, and I am usually with others my age. It feels like we are in a 'camp' experience of some kind, except on board a ship. We only separate when medical procedures are being done. At other times we are being 'taught' lessons to help us be better people here on earth.

They are not 'people' in the sense we are, though they look like us. In their world there is no war. They do not destroy their planet. They do not kill one another. There is no hunger or poverty.

When I am 25 I get married and move to New York City. My desert visits cease; a new life begins for me. Though I am visited sporadically the next four decades, not until I am a 65 year old grandmother will I begin to fully understand who they are, where they come from and what they need from us.

Bronx, NY 2015

It has been three years since I began resurrecting memories of my "visits". I am 68 years old and a grandmother now. Once my first grandchild was born, I began to understand how 'we' were connected to 'them'. I met two types of beings. The taller, human types look very similar to us. The only differences I could ever see were in how their skin seemed to have a muted pigmentation, and how no matter their complexion or hair color their eyes were always on the lighter side; a grey/blue, grey-green or grey/brown.

It is important for me to insert here, that although I have had these visits all my life and have known about these beings, my religious faith has never been shaken. I believe in God. Though I was raised a Christian, I respect all forms of religion that help humankind achieve a better and kinder and more peaceful life. In fact, I tried to tell my priest about my experiences two years ago. He listened and then said, "It's not that I don't believe you." Clearly he did not believe me. Soon after, he was promoted and left our church. We now have a new priest. I am not going to 'tell' him anything. I want to be buried with prayers.

As I resurrected my memories, I began feeling differently about the adolescent abductions. Those years were unlike the first ten, when I was escorted to and from visits and treated like precious cargo. During this next phase, I traveled to and from visits on my own. Sometimes I would awaken as I was being 'energized' back to my room. Many nights I would 'feel' I was falling off a high cliff or ledge. This was a regular happening during my sleep hours as a teenager. Often I felt I was being 'watched or observed' as I slept. I could never see who was watching me. I just knew they 'cared' about me. A feeling of total body paralysis would slowly recede once I was back home. Then, I would sleep deeply.

During this second phase of visits, I was with other teenagers in a 'camp' or school type setting. I remember silently walking with these other adolescents through chilly corridors; we were all in night clothes. One by one we were separated and taken into little rooms where we would undergo medical procedures. The procedures included the taking of ova and, in my case, breast tissue from my right breast. At the end of this decade, I had reconstructive surgery at the age of 20. Every bit of breast tissue in my right breast had been taken. My left breast was fine; my right breast consisted of 'skin' and the nipple area only. My doctors were flummoxed as to what caused this. After the surgery, no more breast tissue was taken by my visitors. However, when I was 23 I believe I was 'pregnant'. After two bewildering months, during which time I never went to a physician as I was ashamed, I awoke in a puddle of blood. I took care of all of this without any medical intervention; I was an unmarried teacher in 1970. I told no one. However, now I believe the embryo might have been taken by my visitors.

Fifty years later, I wondered if I was repressing anger at the violations done to my body. Even though I eventually lost my right ovary to 'unspecified trauma', I could not feel anger towards my visitors for their harvesting of my ova, breast tissue and other DNA. I still cannot feel anger about this. I was a part of them, and they needed something from me which I could give them. I did not consent in our sense of the word; my love and connection to them was the consent. I will justify this harvesting until my dying day. Today, doctors and researchers conduct infinite experiments on other species for the betterment of our own species. Since 'we' are related to them, any research which helps them helps our own descendants.

I was 'marked'.

At age 5, I awoke with a fresh red triangle wound on my upper right thigh. My mother asked me what had happened. I told her I fell off my sister's two wheel bike the day before. She noted the mark had not been there the night before during my bath and took me to a nearby clinic. The young doctor was baffled. He couldn't understand why in so recent an injury there were no stitches. He wanted to know who had first treated the injury. My mother explained that she didn't know how it happened. The young doctor wasn't buying it. In such an injury there would have been copious bleeding. No blood was on me or my bed. He continued to puzzle over the absence of stitches, yet the wound healed perfectly. Mother got me out of there quickly. She had a previous unsettling visit with a doctor when she took me for help with my nosebleeds. My pediatrician, Dr. Thompson, was convinced that I had been taken flying, as I had nasal passages that looked just like those of the pilots he had treated at the nearby airbase. Mother had exited there quickly, as well.

The first few months of my life, mother would often find me on the floor outside my crib, unconscious. She would have to put my head under the faucet to bring me out of whatever state I was in. How I got out of my crib onto the floor, she never discovered. My sister was only a toddler at the time, and my father worked nights. As I always had healthy 'baby' check-ups, my mother let the mystery go. She told me about it decades later, revealing her constant 'fear' of how and why this was happening.

The first two decades of my being visited consisted of my being 'abducted'; however, the last few years were often on a 'voluntary' basis. I was teaching middle school after graduating from the University of Arizona, and once or twice a month (on a Sunday usually) I would drive to a location in the mountain ranges on the outskirts of town. Once there I would park deep in the foothills and check the car clock. My next conscious moment was when I would check the car clock again and find that three hours had passed.

I knew I had been deep inside the mountain, in a clear sarcophagus. While I 'slept' I was given lessons, information and sometimes future glimpses into my life. As I had not always succumbed to the 'knock-out' process when I was a child, I would often awaken during the time in the sarcophagus. Of all my 'visits' and 'experiences' this was among the most jarring. 'They' would put me under again, but the memory of being deep in the huge mountain cavern in the clear sarcophagus is still vivid and unsettling to me. However, it was simply a part of it all...a part of my life.

The transferred information ('lessons') included:

1. They are a part of us; we are a part of them. We always have been and always will be.
2. They cannot understand (and worry about) the wars we wage upon each other.
3. They 'wish' us to help the less fortunate on earth-the hungry and poor on the planet.
4. They 'wish' us to be caretakers of our planet and all the lifeforms on it.
5. They want us to know that though 'evil' exists everywhere, 'good' is more powerful.

After the transfer of lessons, I would be given 'directions' about how to steer my life. Glimpses of future events would pop into my mind for milliseconds.

The future life glimpses had started in 1963, when I was sixteen. Right before the assassination of President Kennedy, I had been shown what would happen to him during what I sometimes remembered as 'daydreams'. I didn't pay much attention to these 'glimpses and premonitions' initially. However, when 'daydreams' would come true, I realized what was happening. After 'seeing' the death of the president, I also saw the death of an uncle, who would die from a shotgun blast (this was Arizona). When I 'saw' that my left arm would be in a cast due to a 3rd degree burn on a certain day, I 'asked' my Bright Friends to take back this ability. I remember standing in my grandfather's small living room. I had rushed over there to take care of him after correctly predicting he was in a health crisis. I was right; he had a stroke. These were too many 'coincidences' for me; I was not prepared to deal with being able to see future events. My 'friends' could not take back the 'gift' because it was simply a part of the visits, which involved time/space anomalies, resulting in these glimpses of future events. I am a civilian and cannot explain how these time/space anomalies occurred. I had to accept it then, as I do now. There still are constant 'glimpses' that I get about certain future events even now. I try not to dwell on them. I prefer to be surprised by life events, especially happy ones.

In one year I will be seventy. I've had a life filled

with joys and sorrows, children and grandchildren and seventy years of visits from those I still call my Bright Friends. I have kept my story and memories to myself for sixty-five years. As I cited previously, it is only during the last three years that I have tried to 'come out of the closet' and share my story and experiences. Besides my unbelieving priest, I told several doctors. My internist, who has known me for over twenty years, said, "Where do you think they come from?" My eye doctor wanted to know about my missing time and a psychiatrist at Mt. Sinai hospital asked me if "I was seeing any of them walking around the hospital corridor." I had consulted the psychiatrist after experiencing high stress levels during my recall sessions. She was almost disappointed that I was not delusional enough to see any Bright Friends or little blue/grey beings walking around the hospital ER.

In addition to over 250 pages of text, I have drawn several dozen scenes. Among my favorites are ones depicting me being taken to the beautiful ship which lit up the surrounding desert darkness; another shows me sitting with one of my little blue/grey friends while a human-looking teacher stands under an arched doorway that is decorated with unusual symbols; yet another represents the youthful messenger who was sent to my bedroom one night to reassure me that I would still be visited if I kept silent about my visits for most of my life.

I have fulfilled my promise to them. I hope now that I will be true to my memories and to the messages and lessons I was given over the decades. They are our descendants. They hold answers to questions about our past and concerns about our future. I also hope that my readers will not be fearful of them, as 'they' wish us no harm. I further hope that readers will open their hearts and minds to the possibility of their existence and to the wonders we will see if we simply open our eyes. I have seen marvelous things, which I cannot explain, but that give me hope tomorrow will surely come. I believe in their goodness; they believe in our goodness and our potential to preserve and deserve our planet. It is as simple and as pure as that. I hope they are right about us.

Karen Kalliopi Papagapitos

There are 225 billion galaxies in
the observable universe

...

www.skyandtelescope

February 2016

Bright Friends: The First Twenty-Five Years of Visitations Tucson, Arizona 1947-1972

by

Karen Kalliopi Papagapitos

"Angel By My Side"

Angel by my side
You've journeyed with me long
Arrived when I was five
Through life you've helped me on

From that first brilliant light
In my still desert room
You transferred words of wisdom
And said you'd be back soon

The years passed by
With joy and pain
With losses and with gain
I felt you near
You eased my fear
And urged push-on again

From that first night
In the bright light
You warned 'speak of this naught,
For you are but a child, and others
will laugh and scoff'

I do not fear to speak out now
Dear angel of the night

xxx

Who came to me in such bright light
And set my child-soul free

And now I wish to thank you
For walking by my side
My roads were full
At times most cruel
You helped me to abide

And so sweet children
If you see an angel in the night
Fear not, the light will lift you
Through life's darkest, hardest plight

(written and published by Karen Kalliopi Papagapitos
2001 in her poetry volume "Artemis Bound')

For my children and their families,
my ancestors and descendants
And, of course, my Bright Friends
And may God help me find the words to
describe the indescribable
...

Prologue

"My friends took me on a ride in the sky last night," I announced to my mother as I walked into the kitchen of our house in Tucson, Arizona. The year was 1951, and I was four years old.

"That's nice," my mother said, smiling to herself at her youngest daughter's over-active imagination.

"The space ship was very shiney. My Bright Friends showed me a picture in my mind of an airplane. The space ship is like our airplanes."

Mother stopped stirring the pot of oatmeal.

"What?" She was walking towards me still holding the wooden spoon covered in oatmeal. Drops of oats were falling on the floor.

"Mommy, what's the 'speed of light' mean?"

Dropping the spoon, my mother knelt down in front of me. Her eyes were level with mine, and I knew she was scared.

"Who are your Bright Friends?"

"They visit me when you and daddy and Tina are all sleeping. You never wake up to see them. They have bright light all around them. It helps them breathe the air here."

I could feel my mother's hands shaking slightly on my shoulders.

"You were just dreaming, Karen."

"No mommy. I could smell the desert around the shiney ship."

"You must never tell anyone else what you have just told me...Never!"

"Mommy, why are you scared?"

"Promise me Karen. Don't tell anyone, ever!"

And then, my nose started to bleed.

ONE NIGHT IN 1951, IN THE QUIET DESERT TOWN OF
TUCSON, ARIZONA - FOUR YEAR OLD KAREN FIRST MET
SOME REMARKABLE INDIVIDUALS. SHE CALLED THEM -

"MY BRIGHT FRIENDS"

"The Decision" by KBP

MY NIGHTTIME FAMILY

PART ONE

THE EARLY YEARS

1-10

I Begin Remembering

I was in someone's arms being carried toward the waiting ship. A hand covered my eyes, seemingly to protect them from the brilliant light. Just ahead of us was the ship. It was beautiful. Bathed in light, it sat on the floor of the desert. I didn't remember how we got to the desert from my room, perhaps I had been sleeping or out from whatever they did to me to make me not remember. However, the brisk early morning air woke me up. I wasn't afraid; I knew these 'friends'. They came for me often.

They must have known I was awake because suddenly a communication was 'sent' to me. A picture of one of 'our' airplanes flashed in my mind. The message that accompanied it was, "It's like an airplane," referring to their ship. All our communication was of this type, a non-verbal ping-pong game of sending and receiving thoughts, emotions, etc. Although I was just three or four years of age and had never seen an airplane, I 'knew' what they meant. The communication was extremely clear.

We began walking up the gangplank. Once inside I was put down. I excitedly ran from room to room, asking if we were going to play the same 'games' we did last time. They exchanged glances with one another. They knew I was remembering. For whatever reason, they decided to keep visiting me a few more times before finally sending a 'messenger' to me one night to decide whether or not our visits should continue.

From the moment I began remembering, I knew I loved these gentle Bright Friends. There were two groups or types of them. One group looked like us; human height, physique, limbs, facial features, ears, hair, etc. They were dressed in very soft luminescent clothing. The ones in the infirmary wore all white, always. The 'teachers' in the little classroom wore white and blue, and the pilots wore white and green. Then there were the shorter ones. To me they looked like other children. They had arms and legs, but their heads were slightly larger in proportion to their bodies than the 'others' heads were to their bodies. They had eyes, a small mouth and nose. I couldn't see their ears because they wore little caps. Their skin was different from the skin of the other type. The little ones had a blue or grey 'hue' to their skin. They all dressed alike in little overalls and shirts. Even their hands were covered. A bright light surrounded the 'human looking' types when they were out of the ship's environment, such as in the desert or my room. When we were all in the ship, there was no bright light. It helped them 'breathe' was what I was made to understand. The little ones wore a hazmat type mask when they were in the desert or my room. They didn't always need the bright light around them.

Even though the two groups were different in appearance, they had the same thoughts and 'souls'. Both groups were gentle, kind and benevolent. They both loved to laugh and treated me like precious cargo. From early on I felt a deep connection with all of my visitors. I would cry when it came time to take me back. I never stopped 'asking' them (non-verbally) if I could live with them. Whenever we parted, I could 'feel' their enormous sadness, as well. I knew they loved me as much as I loved them. Sixty-five years later, I would 'relive' our sadness and pain in parting with my first granddaughter, whenever I had to leave her after a visit. It would be a moment of clarity to me as to what our genetic tie was and what our 'relationship' to each other really was. It would be a simple, profound truth.

I did not tell my mother about every visit. They were such a natural part of my life, I assumed she knew. After one particularly exciting flight, I went to her the next morning and tried to describe what had happened.

"I know how day comes," I told her. "There's a big boom and then it's day...just like that." Apparently, the ship broke the sound barrier when it 'jumped' from location to location. We had journeyed from the southern Arizona desert night to an area on earth that had already seen the sun rise. To me, the coming of day happened just like I described to my mother. She was unimpressed.

"You were dreaming," she said continuing her ironing.

"Mommy, what's the sound barrier?"

Mother stopped ironing. She knew I wasn't making all these stories up. There was too much scientific detail for a very young child to improvise. Again, she kneeled down so that she was level with me. She hugged me tightly, whispering in my ear to...

"Never tell anyone. Never tell...".

Tucson, Arizona 1947-1972

Today Tucson, Arizona has a population of over half a million people. In 1947, thirty-five years after Arizona became a state in 1912 and the year of my birth, the population of Tucson was 50,000. The Colorado River Project that would transform hundreds of arid desert acres into lush golf ranges was still fifteen years away.

Tucson got its name from local Native American people who had inhabited the area for centuries. Its literal translation means, "at the foot of the black mountain." This was a logical name to identify the budding pueblo that was in a valley surrounded by four mountain ranges. Today, as it was in the 1950s, the names of the mountain ranges are the Tucson mountains to the NW of town, the Santa Rita range to the SW, the Rincon range to the SE and the Catalina range to the NE. Before GPS, when I was a young woman driving to my first teaching assignments, I would use the mountains as navigational markers. Everyone did who had grown up in the area. If you were guided by the surrounding mountains, you would never get lost. Sixty miles to the south of Tucson, Arizona is the border town of Nogales, Arizona. Across the border is her sister town of Nogales, Sonora.

As a young child growing up in the untamed desert surrounding Tucson, I was exposed to a multi-cultural mecca comprised mainly of Hispanic, Native American and European inhabitants. By the time I began school in 1953, Asians and African Americans were also beginning to establish roots in Tucson. I had multi-cultural friends to the credit of my parents who viewed everyone as fairly as they could considering their isolated upbringing in Greek and Greek American culture.

My father was born in Greece, near Tripoli, in 1905 and didn't come to America until 1940. My maternal grandmother, Kalliopi, came to America in 1913 with her brothers from the tiny hamlet of Hania, Crete. She met my grandfather, Haralambos, shortly after arriving and they married. My mother, Athena, was their first child. My other grandparents, Nicholas and Christina, died in the village of Tziba, near Tripoli before I could meet them. I carry their story in the wonderful oral history my father gave to me.

Although my parents married in Akron, Ohio a move to a warmer, drier climate was recommended as my father had weak lungs. One doctor suggested Tucson, Arizona. My father took an exploratory trip in 1942 and immediately identified with the desert terrain and surrounding mountains reminiscent of his origins in Greece. My mother and infant sister followed in 1946 and the following year I was born.

My parents opened a restaurant in the early 1950s between Congress Street and Broadway on South Fourth Ave. They named it the LaSalle and it was immediately successful. Although I think the bar that my aunt and uncle operated next door had a great deal to do with that. In addition, the illegal gambling with 'bookies' that went on in the back booths soon established the LaSalle as the go to place for food and fun.

Because my parents were typically conservative Europeans who kept their children as close as they could, they built a small apartment in the back of the restaurant. This allowed them to awaken us early weekend mornings, about 4am, so that they could open the LaSalle for the truckers who relied on coffee and pastry to keep them going. I remember those sleepy, early morning walks to our 1944 model Cadillac. The smell of the early morning desert was drenched with dew filled promises of burgeoning life. I will never forget that smell.

Tucson remained quaint and territorial throughout the 1950s. However, the snowbird trade bringing easterners to the comforting warmth of the desert in January and February was exploding. After the Colorado River Project in the 1960s came to fruition, golf ranges began sprouting up in the previously inhospitable desert. Dude ranches gave way to luxury snowbird resorts. An era was ending and a new one beginning.

By the time I became a teacher, migrant workers filled the ripe fields to the south of Tucson. One of my last teaching assignments was as a first grade teacher in a tiny school system in Continental, Arizona. It was so small it only had trailers for classrooms. Both the children of migrants and the children of ranchers attended. Fortunately, at that time I could speak some Spanish. I vowed to treat all the children as equals and encouraged bilingualism in the classroom. Two decades later, I would publish two children's books ('Jose's Basket' and 'Socorro, Daughter of the Desert') as a tribute to the courageous migrant children I had taught.

I loved the desert with every inch of my heart. I never considered leaving it. Fate intervened when I met my future husband, while visiting a friend in Los Angeles, California. He was a businessman from New York. Less than six months after our initial meeting, I would be married in New York City. The day I flew away over my GPS mountains was both painful and full of promise. I could see our future children in my fiance's eyes. However, I was not only leaving the desert. I was leaving the Bright Friends who had been a constant part of my life for the past 25 years. What I didn't realize at the time was that they were not leaving me.

The Ship: My First Impressions

My first memories of being taken aboard the ship started when I was three or four years of age. My Bright Friends would arrive in my bedroom without waking anyone else up. It looked like the wall just 'melted away' and they could walk through it to me. In later years, during the second adolescent phase, I would see this happen in the corridors of larger ships, as my group would gain entry into an examination room. For now, in my child's mind, the wall between my bedroom and our back yard simply 'melted' to allow them to walk through.

From my back yard we 'jumped' to the waiting ship, in the isolated desert surrounding town. I only have a human vocabulary beginning in 1947 to describe an indescribable event. As we stood in my back yard, I was in the arms of one of my visitors, and the brilliant light surrounding my friends also surrounded me. The next thing I knew there was a whoosh accompanied by a 'shudder' and we were in the desert with the ship.

The brilliant light surrounding the ship was the brightest I can remember. Because it covered such a large area the intensity was amplified. The Bright Friend who was holding me covered my eyes to protect them. I still kept them opened and would look over his hand so as not to miss anything. We began to approach the gang plank to enter the ship which stood a few feet off the ground. It was not perfectly round but more elliptical. It resembled two plates, one inverted on top of the other with a space in between. In the space separating the two parts different lights emanated. Years later in my teens I would panic at railroad crossings because the blinking lights reminded me of the ship powering up for us to take off. My friends had always emphasized that we be secured in our protective 'seats' before this could occur. Once we were airborne, I was allowed to roam about. Because it was so critical to them that I be secured in my special reclining chair before we took off, I carried that intense 'rule' with me into adolescence and transferred it to the blinking red and blue lights at the railroad crossings. My mother, who usually would be driving me in the daytime, never understood my panic. She thought I didn't trust her, and I didn't. I just couldn't explain why to her.

In those early years, the ships they used were not the largest in their fleet. It seemed large to me since I was so small. Once inside, and before they secured me in my special chair, I would run about excited to see everything again. My favorite room was the little 'classroom or playroom'. All the walls in the ship's interior were light grey/blue. Oval portholes were in every room but not always opened. For take-off they were usually closed. Different writing, not our alphabet but a combination of strange letters and geometric shapes, identified each room. These were over doorway arches that led to the different parts of the ship.

When my nose would bleed I would be taken to the infirmary and put on the examination table. Two doctors would try to stop the blood. They were dressed in white and were always very concerned when my nose began to bleed. I showed them how I could hold my head back and pinch my nose to keep the blood from dripping down my nightgown. They would smile at me whenever I did this and I could feel their affection for me. I can still taste the coppery blood flowing down my throat. Eventually, if the blood did not stop, they would spray something deep in my nose. After a nosebleed I was always given a sweet drink and a biscuit of some kind. The closest I can come to describing the taste of both would be a honey nectar flavor. To this day I love syrup of any kind and have an insatiable sweet tooth.

Beside the classroom/playroom with its little table, chairs and colorful 'toys' and the infirmary, there was the bridge and an atrium. The atrium held plant cuttings and rock or gem samples taken from the desert. I loved going in there, and my Bright Friends would try to explain what each sample was. Most were collected by the shorter, different looking ones. They were the ones who tended the atrium making sure each cutting or gem sample was stored properly until the crew got them home safely.

A highlight of every trip was being taken to the bridge during some of the flight. This happened after my time in the little classroom/playroom was over. I would be allowed to stand on a ledge near the porthole. As we traveled or jumped from place to place I could see the clouds surrounding the ship. We often flew with cloud cover and I sometimes thought it was raining outside because of the moisture on the outside of the portholes from the clouds.

When I first saw the ship, one of my Bright Friends conveyed the message that it was 'like our airplanes'. A picture of an airplane appeared inside my mind. I had never seen an airplane, but when they showed me how they flew I understood the comparison. During subsequent flights it was 'explained' to me, all non-verbally, that the ship usually didn't fly in straight lines. It would jump from location to location, or hover in one spot. Only if traveling in a straight line was recommended did they utilize this flight pattern. I now believe it was because flying in straight lines would be more visible to the residents (us) below. Unless someone had been cleared for knowledge of their existence, they usually tried to cover their presence on earth.

My Bright Friends were kind, benevolent, wise

individuals who wanted to 'help' us. It was always communicated that 'we' were related (they and us). We were family. Indeed, growing up those early years I felt I had two families: my parents and sister comprised one and my Bright Friends the other. Both were equally loved by me and still are.

A NOSEBLEED! AGAIN
1950

The Early Years

"The Nosebleeds, Triangle Mark and Doctor Visits"

When the visits became more frequent so did my nosebleeds. Their intensity increased as well. Often my parents didn't know what to do. I was a thin little girl and a very picky eater. Soon, the blood loss took a toll and I became weak. A simple blood test established I was anemic, and I was prescribed chocolate flavored iron tablets that I was to chew. I was too young to swallow pills. The lab technicians told mother to keep them in the refrigerator. I still remember the cold, chalky aftertaste. I am amazed that I still like chocolate. In addition to the chalky chocolate iron tablets, I had to have weekly blood tests from both my finger tips and my veins. Mother didn't stop there, though. She wanted to know 'why' I was getting nosebleeds. According to my parents, nobody on either side ever had trouble with them. So, she took me to my elderly pediatrician.

Dr. T. had treated me from birth. He knew my ear, nose and throat anatomy better than anyone, as I would get frequent ear infections.

"Has Karen been in an airplane recently?" He asked my mother, while checking and rechecking my nasal passages and ear canals.

"Of course not doctor. No one in our family has been in an airplane. Vasily (my father) drives us everywhere."

I could see my mother was uncomfortable answering his question, as only a few weeks had passed since I had told her about my Bright Friends and the night flights they took me on in the sky. I didn't say anything because my mother had lollipops in her purse. She had promised me I could have more than one if I didn't say anything about my visitors. I wanted the candy, and so I kept silent.

"Why are you asking that?" my mother pressed.

"Her nasal passages look just like the nasal passages of the pilots I treat out at the airbase south of town. It looks like she has been exposed to differences in barometric pressure. A lot of the pilots I treat are having trouble with nose bleeds as well, now that their speeds can break the sound barrier."

That did it for mother. She thanked the doctor, pulled me off the table and got the hell out of there.

Her doctor troubles were not yet over.

Soon after, I awoke one morning with a red wound high on the front of my right thigh.

"Where did this come from?" Mother asked staring at the angry red triangle mark. There was a little dip in the center of the triangle, as if a bit of flesh had been removed.

"I fell off Tina's bike, remember mama?" I had a

memory of trying to ride my sister's two wheel bike the previous afternoon. In the memory, my mother was sitting on our back stoop steps. Also in the memory, she had made no effort to help me with my wound. Somehow the memory made sense to me.

"It wasn't there last night," mother said. She was worried about it getting infected, so she took me to a nearby clinic. After her last encounter with Dr. T., she didn't want to risk me blabbing about flying in the midnight sky with brilliantly lit up friends.

"How did you say your daughter got this and when?" A young doctor was looking intently at the wound.

"Karen said she fell off her sister's two wheel bicycle yesterday. I don't remember seeing it last night during her bath. Karen's not able to ride a two wheeler yet, she's too young." Mother seemed confused.

"This is a deliberate surgical excision of tissue made by a very sharp, precise instrument. How did this skin flap close without stitches?" the young doctor was shaking his head while looking at the mark with a magnifying glass. There was a skin flap covering the dip in the middle of the red triangle. It looked like it had 'pressed' itself shut.

Mother became quiet. First were my damaged nasal passages and now a mysterious surgical mark appeared on my leg. Someone was hurting her daughter. I could tell she was very frightened.

"I'd like another doctor to examine it."

"Look doctor," mother came to the point, "all I need to know is if it's infected."

"It's not infected. It's perfect. Just keep it clean and dry for a day or two and come back if anything changes." He turned to go, and then...

"Karen, how did you get this mark?" he directed his question to me. I looked at my scared mother.

"Tina's bike fell on me. I didn't show mommy so she wouldn't get mad at me." I improvised for both our sakes. The young doctor seemed temporarily mollified and mother rushed me out of there. On our way out of the clinic, mother turned to me.

"Thank you, Karen." We both knew something was wrong because our stories didn't match. It didn't matter. I trusted my friends and mother trusted me.

That night, independent of one another, my father was never told about my mysterious triangle mark. It remained an unspoken secret between my mother and me until it had healed and the redness disappeared. However, my mother now knew that something highly unusual was happening to me. She didn't know what and she didn't seem eager to find out.

The Messenger Visits

My family was very religious. I was baptized a Greek Orthodox Christian shortly after my birth in 1947. There were many beautiful Catholic churches in Tucson in 1947, but not a Greek Orthodox church. My parents took me to Phoenix for the ceremony. Once we had our own church in Tucson, my parents took my sister and me every Sunday morning for services. Even as very young children we fasted completely before taking the sacrament of Communion during the liturgy. Many times, being the frail child I was, I would throw up from no food or water before taking the sacrament. I didn't mind. I loved God and wanted to please Him. The church we attended had been built by my father and his friends, with the help of local laborers. It was filled inside with icons depicting Jesus, the Virgin Mary and the saints in soft clothing with bright light around them. I saw these icons every Sunday of my young life.

I was four years old when a messenger was sent to me. I awakened in the early hours after midnight to find one of my brilliantly lit up friends seated near the foot of my bed. He wasn't wearing the clothing members of the crew usually wore. It was still luminescent, but he had more 'layers' on. He had light brown hair and seemed to be no older than thirty (of our years). Once again he began communicating in the non-verbal, mental imaging way.

'We do not know why you are remembering our visits, but you are. People usually don't remember being visited.' Was his first communication.

I just listened, without replying. He continued.

'We are not sure whether we should continue to visit you. We might have to stop.'

I began to cry hysterically. It was exactly as if one of my parents had told me they were going away never to see me again.

'If you tell people about your visits, they will tell you that it is only a dream.'

I knew he was right; my mother kept saying I was dreaming when I tried to tell her about them.

'It would be better if you did not tell anyone. Can you do that?'

I sent him a big 'yes' and stopped crying.

'We want you to know that you are not dreaming. These visits are really happening.'

I showed him a picture in his mind of me smelling the desert as we boarded the ship, so he would know I knew it was really happening. He smiled.

'We are related; your people and us. We are family. You will understand many years from now.'

'Will you still visit me?' I asked him.

'Yes.' He replied. Without realizing it, he sent me a message that was not part of the official one.

'You are fortunate.'

Then, he was gone.

I fell back to sleep instantly, content in the knowledge that my Bright Friends would still visit me. This one night is an extremely vivid memory, as I was allowed to be fully awake. At no time did any of my Bright Friends identify themselves to me with specific names. It didn't matter. I knew each one of this core group intimately. Even though the brilliant light that surrounded the young messenger in my dark bedroom had reminded me of the icons in church, I knew these visitors weren't God. I also knew something else. They weren't people. The messenger had communicated that 'people' usually don't remember. This meant that they were not people like we were, even though some of them looked just like us. I was very young, but the clarity of the communication allowed me to grasp certain truths.

Sixty years later, when I became a grandmother, I had an epiphany about my connection to them. I realized the sadness I felt when parting from my toddler granddaughter was exactly the same as the sadness I had felt when I parted from my Bright Friends after a visit. It was what Oprah would call an 'aha moment'. Once I made this analogy, I realized that my(our) connection with the visitors was a result of many generations of interaction. Soon, memories that had previously been blocked would begin flooding back.

I was true to my promise and never said anything else to anyone throughout my childhood. Not until six decades later, after my 'aha moment' would I begin to share my memories. I know I do not write about them objectively. It is impossible for me to separate my feelings when I write. They were benevolent and kind. They were trying to help us live better lives. We weren't supposed to remember. Only I did.

‘My Sister and the Others’

At all times during these early years, my visitors, those I called Bright Friends, made every effort to keep me safe, happy and unafraid during our time together. Only once do I remember my sister being in the little classroom/playroom with me. Every other time I was on the ship my sister wasn’t there. If they were going to visit her, it would have been with me. Time is just as important to them as to us. In 1950, the year I began remembering, the desert surrounding Tucson was quiet and completely dark. The proximity of the airbase south of town helped cover-up many sightings. However, the night sky over Tucson’s desert was a background of blue/black velvet covered with diamond-like stars. It was hard not to look up at this beautiful sight. My Bright Friends had to limit their visits; therefore if my sister was to be visited, it would have been with me.

If they could, my visitors answered my questions to them. When I began inquiring as to why my sister hadn’t come with me, they showed me a picture in my mind of her being very scared and having bad dreams after the first few times they had tried to include her. I believe I was the primary subject, as I was born in the desert in 1947 and could be tracked from birth in their observations and studies. Also, I was a full-term baby, born after a 9 month gestation. My sister, born in Ohio, had been two months premature and did not have contact with my mother for two weeks after her birth. She had been in an incubator until her birth weight increased. She might not have been qualified for long term study. In the end, I was the 'smart monkey', and I write that with love and affection. I thrived on the visitations.

As the messenger who had been sent to my room communicated to me, 'I was fortunate.' Indeed, I was fortunate on many levels. I have thought about this often since I began work on this memoir. First, by accident of birth I was not born into a family that was burdened with the chains of poverty. My parents owned their own business, and although it had not made them wealthy, they were rich in every way possible. They owned their own home; my sister and I were healthy, and we were of European background; a factor that eased our life in the conservative southern Arizona community of 1947-1957.

I was 'fortunate' that my visits continued with this benevolent, good group of visitors. Much later, in the final few years of my visitations, I learned that although I had been 'chosen' by a benevolent, well-intentioned (toward humanity) group, there were 'others' who were not as well-intentioned. The methods of this other group were not as caring; they took people whenever they needed to without clearance from any official group and they did not treat them with the care and love that my visitors treated me. This explains the disparity between my experiences and the experiences of many abductees who come away traumatized for life by their encounters. However, from what information I was given during the later years, these visitors operate on an illegal pirate status and are fugitives in their world. They usually are being hunted by their own militia. They also are not in the majority. As I now know, they contribute to the mistaken idea that all alien visitors are alike: cold, cruel and non-caring individuals who frighten helpless abductees. Had my visits not continued and my 'protective status' terminated, I would have been at the mercy of these 'others'. This possibility pressured my Bright Friends to keep visiting me; only in this way was I protected. The triangle mark, which today is so faded the naked eye cannot see it, sent a clear message to any other group that might have tried to visit me. The consequences of such an attempt would be dire and punishment for the offense would be severe. I believe a tracking device was implanted, possibly in my nose or skull. It would have alerted my Bright Friends if others took me and did not return me immediately upon seeing the triangle mark. With my current knowledge of how many other people describe their horrifying experiences, I continue to be grateful to my benevolent visitors.

I try not to watch many television shows about other abductees. The way the 'little visitors' are portrayed is upsetting to me given my experiences. They are described as monsters who want to enslave us and train us for global warfare. I find this unreasonable. The 'others', although operating on an illegal uncaring level, would not want to destroy us or our planet. The information and samples obtained from abductions (in my case 'visitations') are valuable imports for their world. If I do watch a show wherein someone describes their experience, including how the visitors told them their 'names' and had sexual relations with them, then either they are lying or embellishing their abduction.

Of one thing I am certain, my Bright Friends did not visit them.

"Growing Up in the Desert"

During those early years, the desert surrounding Tucson was undeveloped and raw; its beauty stark against the backdrop of the four mountain ranges that encircled the valley in which the town nested. Miles elementary school, which was directly across from our house on Broadway and Highland Avenue, included desert survival skills in the curriculum, should we ever get lost in the desert. We were to drink our urine, eat the pods from a prickly pear cactus, never overturn a rock in the daytime in case a snake was sleeping beneath it, try to find cover and if we had crayons on us we should eat them. If we had the bad luck to be bitten by a rattlesnake or copperhead snake, both very poisonous, it was recommended we make an X mark with a knife (which we should always have on us during desert outings), suck the venom from the wound and then immediately spit it out. Salt tablets were to be carried at all times and ingested as needed. Head cover was mandatory and a canteen with water preferable. In case a horse was with us, we were to share the water and salt tablets with them. The horse would know what to eat on its own.

Rounding out our survivalist education were visits from the staff of the Arizona Living Desert Museum situated in the untamed desert southwest of town.

Young biologists who worked at the museum while attending the University of Arizona would bring snakes, gila monsters, tarantulas, scorpions, prairie dogs (a favorite as they were cute little rodents that resembled unkempt squirrels), etc. We were taught the proper way to hold a snake so that it could not bite you or squeeze you to death. If there was a forked branch near you, so much the better. It could be used to pin and hold the snake's dangerous head. If not, we were instructed to swiftly grab it directly behind the head with a firm a grip and then at the end of the tail, again firmly. I don't remember what we were supposed to do with the snake once we were holding it.

My parents would send us to 'ranch camp' during the summer months. We were taught how to ride horses, as well as how to feed them with a flat hand and how never to stand behind a horse because they could kick you. Also included in the activities was how to load and shoot a rifle. I can still feel the butt of the rifle press against my shoulder. My arms would ache from trying to steady the incredibly heavy armament while also trying to aim at the target. Rifle practice was in the morning and archery was in the afternoon. Again my little arms would ache after an hour of trying to not only hold the heavy bow while placing the arrow correctly plus trying to aim properly, but we also had to have strung it correctly before doing any of the above.

A favorite part of the day was grooming and riding the horses. They weren't polished English steeds, but rather dusty mares and studs that patiently stood while little hands brushed them and tried to put a blanket and saddle on their backs. They must have taken pity on us as they never threw us. A love of horses and riding has stayed with me throughout my life. An unfulfilled dream of mine is to be riding a horse in the annual February parade through the old part of Tucson. As children, my sister and I stood with the crowds and watched as the sheriffs and deputies rode past. Even the smell of the manure was not bad, as the horses ate hay.

By the time I was nine years of age, my parents had sold the original LaSalle on Fourth Ave. and moved to south Congress Street. The new restaurant was closer to the judicial part of town. Lawyers and judges were steady lunchtime customers, which was handy when one of their workers landed in jail for being drunk and disorderly.

My father loved all kinds of sports. Often he would take me to the wrestling matches, when the boyfriends of our pretty waitresses were scheduled. He also took me to boxing matches and the spring training of the Cleveland Indians baseball team. My sister had no interest in joining us, but I went because

I got the best hot dogs at the ball park. Curiously, in her free time, mother took us to revival meetings in tents on the outskirts of town. We were sworn to secrecy not to tell my father. Perhaps she went in her search to find out what was happening to me. Mother also took me, not my sister, to visits with Catholic nuns and the Rabbi at the one temple in Tucson at the time. She didn't explain why she took me, however in retrospect searching for answers seems as good a reason as any.

Of course, we still went to church and Sunday school regularly. Afternoon Greek school lessons trumped Brownies and Girl Scouts. It was a busy, happy time. It was a time of innocence. I had not yet learned of the horrors in the world or of what unspeakable acts we were capable of. The world and my Bright Friends would educate me in later years. Back then, the desert was a place of beauty and adventure and, of course, a place where I met my wonderful visitors for magical night rides.

DESERT SKY, DESERT SAND

I was born under a desert sky
where stars lit up the night
The moon was there
amid fair shares
of diamonds, clear and bright

Night's silky sand, soft on warm earth
awaited desert's sun
With colors rare, to greet light's birth
this land and I were one

Then Fate gave call;
my heart took pause
For from this land I loved
I had to go far to the North
My time to leave had come

Soon Cityscapes
and concrete peaks
replaced my homesick hues
of desert skies and diamond stars
Hard-pressed I bartered views

It took some years, and many tears,
for me to realize
that anyplace can boast, as well
of skies and dawn's new rise

Now life's complete
and well I know what holds
stars, sky and sand
It's love, not land, that
fills our hearts
And holds us in its hand

"They Were A Part of A Whole"

They were humble. They communicated that they were a part of something larger; we all were. We were related. We were family.

Even as a child I could sense their humility. Although a sense of individuality existed in particular with the group that resembled us, it was just that…a characteristic rather than driving force. Just as regularly as they would communicate the 'we were related' message, they also communicated that everyone, both they and us, were a part of something larger. A picture of a huge, vast system came into my mind. Some trips were devoted to having me understand this.

Games we played in the little classroom/playroom often had me putting little dolls representing my family in order. Dolls representing the different races on earth followed and put around the dolls of my family. Following that, dolls representing both of the groups that were visiting me were placed around all of the other dolls. We did the same with representations of the earth and sun, other solar systems, other galaxies, and so on. I was learning that everything existed in relation to something else. No one existed independently of others. It was 'the no man is an island' lesson.

Of course, what my Bright Friends knew but didn't share with me was that our egos were causing problems. We had just come out of World War II, where humanity had to stand up to regimes that were trying to erase entire populations and races because of misguided bigotry. It was financially appealing, as well, however the main reason given the citizens of the warring nations was an 'ethnic cleansing' one. Good people followed fanatic leaders to horrific ends. After the war was over, these same citizens were taken on tours of the concentration camp atrocities. Not many could keep their eyes open and view the skeletal remains of men, women and children heaped into piles like so much trash. Rooms full of gold taken from jewelry and the teeth of the victims clearly indicated what the real intent was. It was a simple case of greed and ego that had been translated into a war of eugenics so that a deluded populous would follow them blindly.

In future years, approximately two decades after leaving the desert, I would write a children's book titled "Socorro, Daughter of the Desert". Socorro, a young migrant girl, was helping look after her small brothers when she encountered a phantom in the desert. As he motioned her away from a large rock, Socorro saw the rattlesnake waiting to strike. The next time the phantom appeared it warned her mother and other migrant workers not to drink from a malaria contaminated well. After more warnings that saved people from imminent danger, Socorro knew that the phantom was a benevolent one. She also knew something else. He was just a part of the desert; just like they all were. What I didn't realize was that I was weaving lessons I had been taught by my Bright Friends into my story.

I envision a future world when we will be able to dissolve our egos just as my visitors dissolved walls so that they could enter my room at night. Only by letting go of our egos will we be able to 'see' a larger picture. People the world round try to do the right thing. We build wells, send seeds and medicines to underdeveloped and poverty stricken communities and dispatch members of WHO when epidemics break out. However, the reality that children and their families worldwide continue to toil for a simple meal continues. Diamonds in Africa are often the product of just such labor. The diamonds finally make their way to pristine window displays where the wealthy can purchase them guilt free.

That still doesn't erase the reality.

I am a faulted human. Although I have tried to live a 'clean' life, during some periods of my life acquiring material possessions became a goal rather than a treat or reward. I am ashamed of those years. However, had I not fallen victim to my inner greed I would not be able to arrive at my present peace at this stage of my life. I hope I never return to a greed-driven, status oriented life again. I now think about children whose stomachs ache from hunger and who are shivering for lack of heat. If I live through my seventies, I hope to make a contribution to those who continue struggling simply to survive. To do this, I must lose sight of borders and boundaries.

If we, citizens of earth, ever want to communicate with our visitors we must find a common language on our own planet first; not a language of words but one of intent. When we can look upon our brothers and sisters across cultural and geographical borders without fear and with love, and accept that we all are a part of a greater whole...then we will be ready. Prophets and spiritual leaders from times long past have told us as much.

My Bright Friends and I were a part of the desert. That desert was a part of the world. That world was a part of a greater system. I am a tiny part of it all.

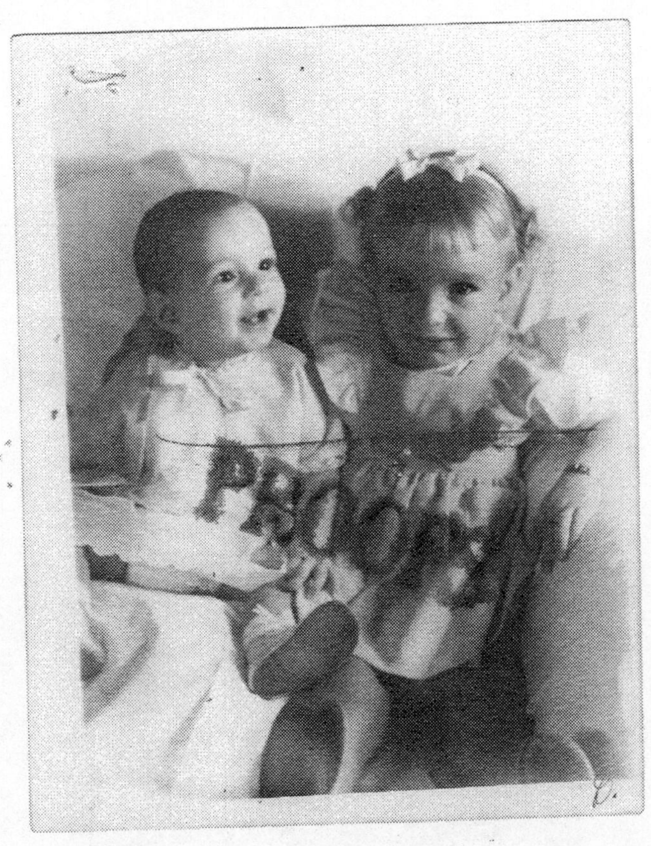

NOVEMBER 1947 TUCSON, ARIZONA
KALLIOPI AT 6 MONTHS OF AGE
HER SISTER CHRISTINA 2½ YEARS OF AGE
(TINA)

"NIGHT FLIGHT" KBP

"A Journey In The Orb Of Light"

TUCSON, ARIZONA 1951
A VISIT TO THE PEDIATRICIAN BECAUSE OF THE NOSEBLEEDS

TUCSON, ARIZONA 1965
KALLIOPI AGE 18 YEARS

HOSPITAL
10/4/13
ESCAPING THE HOSPITAL

HANIA, CRETE
1925

Top Left: PAVLOS MANOSOUDAKIS
MY GREAT-GRANDFATHER

ATHENA MANOSOVDAKIS
MY GREAT GRANDMOTHER

AKRON, OHIO 1923

MY PAPU
(GRANDFATHER)
HARALAMBOS CHRISTOPOULOS

THE CHILDREN
(from LEFT TO RIGHT)
MY UNCLE PAUL (3 YEARS)
MY MOTHER ATHENA (7 YEARS)
MY AUNT ANNIE (2 YEARS)
MY AUNT SOPHIA (5 YEARS)

MY YIAYIA
(GRANDMOTHER)
KALLIOPI CHRISTOPOULOS
6 MONTHS PREGNANT WITH TWIN BOYS

THE AUTHOR'S PARENTS VASILY AND ATHENA
ON THEIR WEDDING DAY
MARCH 2nd, 1941
AKRON, OHIO

TUCSON, ARIZONA 1972 KALLIOPI
AT 25 YEARS OF AGE

"Bright Friends: The First Twenty-Five Years..."

Part One: The Early Years (1-10)
'Goodbye For Now'

As a child, I tried to tell my mother about my Bright Friends and our time together. In later years, my mother told me about the mornings she would find me on the floor outside my crib. She would frantically try to awaken me, finally taking me to the kitchen sink and running cold water on my face. I was six months old, and apparently this happened more than once. She knew something was different in how I experienced the world, she just couldn't explain it. The years passed and since promising my visitors that I wouldn't tell anyone, I remained silent when questioned by her. I believe this was why she took me to revival meetings, to Rabbis and to the Catholic nuns. She was seeking answers to impossible questions. I am now a mother and grandmother and can understand her then constant maternal concern.

I have tender memories of the time I spent with my Bright Friends. They remained baffled by my ability to bypass their efforts in blocking my memories of our experiences. As the young messenger had communicated to me,

"We don't know why you are remembering. People usually don't remember."

When I see depictions of the 'grays' drawn from abductee witness accounts, I do not recognize their facial expressions. In the pictures, the artists have drawn monster-like aliens with menacing black eyes. My little friends, the small ones I believed to be children, did not have those expressions. Their eyes were not menacing and never had I sensed any evil intentions emanating from them. Both the smaller ones and the ones that looked like us were benevolent, kind and wise. They had a wonderful sense of humor. I remember us laughing over something funny often.

It seems we want to perpetuate an evil alien agenda and lump all visitors into this one category. Although I only encountered two types of visitors, I have no doubt that many different groups exist in their world; just as many different races of humans exist in ours. It appears that great effort is put into making us believe they all look alike, and they all are evil with their ultimate goals being our enslavement or their domination of earth. To this I can only steer my readers to the global evidence of alien visitations to earth from our earliest origins. Even if we (human/alien hybrids) were initially bred as a work force to mine the precious metals and other natural resources on earth, why are the aliens not waging global warfare with their superior technology and be done with it? I am not discounting that some types or groups of aliens are ill-intentioned, however as my Bright Friends communicated to me, the benevolent ones were more powerful than the ill-intentioned ones.

There were never any lessons about God or religion specifically. Yet throughout these early years and woven into other lessons was a subtle respect for all religions in general. In later years and lessons, this would be communicated in more sophisticated ways. During the early years it was made clear to me that they were not God; they were like us. We were related. We were family. They were humble.

My Bright Friends would work in 'messages' while I played or was taken to the bridge to watch parts of a flight, or to the atrium where the gems were stored. They taught me about the crystalline make-up of the samples and what they were used for in their world and ours. Instead of communicating that they were not a part of our world, I learned quite the opposite from them. Recurring themes to lessons were that 'they were a part of our world, just as we were a part of their world'. Everything was connected to everything else. I remember one lesson when they tried to explain how many years old their world was compared to earth. They used mirrors. One mirror reflected another mirror, then that mirror reflected the original mirror, ad infinitum. I came away from the experience with a basic understanding of time passing. The lesson was aided by their incredibly superior non-verbal communication. Although I was a small child, I was able to grasp the basics of the lesson. My ability to communicate with them effectively was one of the reasons they wanted to continue our visits.

After I reached my tenth birthday our visits began to taper off. Then came a devastating communication: they wouldn't be able to visit me for a while. I was heartbroken, and so were they. I would soon reach puberty. I would be moving on to different types of visitation. I could sense this initial group of Bright Friends was worried about me. They never communicated why. They did let me know that one or more of them would watch over me during this time, whenever they could. There was one in particular that seemed especially bonded to me. He had sandy hair and gray eyes. He is the one I have drawn with me against the simple backdrop of the mountain. He was the one who would watch over me sleeping, after I was brought back from a future harvesting visit.

My mother and teachers knew I was upset. When my teachers asked me what was wrong, I told them my family was going away. They questioned my mother; she denied it. The recommendation was that she meet me every day after school as reassurance she had not left. They decided I was a typically hormonal prepubescent girl. I silently bore my sorrow, believing what had been promised. I would see them again. That was all that mattered. They would come back to me. They had promised.

"UNDER THE LAKE"

"NIGHT BECOMES DAY!"

the Nazca lines in the Ingenio Valley
of Peru date back to 200 BC

...

If the local population wasn't using
this ancient airway, who was?

www.go2peru.com

PART TWO

THE HARVESTING YEARS

11-19

'The Harvesting Begins'

It was happening again. I couldn't move a muscle. I couldn't make a sound. I was not afraid. This happened often. Right before this temporary paralysis, I could feel myself falling through dark space. I was not alone.

He was there, standing by my bed watching me. I could feel his love for me.

'Why are you here again?' I would ask through my thoughts to him.

'Just sleep now,' was his soft thought back

A short time before my ova and breast tissue had been harvested.

It was alright.

My Bright Friend was here.

I was tired, so tired.

'Sleep' his soft thought repeated.

'Yiayia Kalliopi'

In 1958 my grandmother died. I was her namesake, Kalliopi, though my mother had Americanized it to Karen when I started first grade. Yiayia had been blind for five years prior to her death, from glaucoma according to the doctors who treated her. My grandmother had another theory. The tears she had shed while my uncle Paul was a prisoner of war from 1943-44 were the real reason. Her blindness did not stop her from baking bread every Sunday, as well as making lamb and Greek potatoes for her grandchildren to enjoy after church. My grandfather, papu Haralambos, and yiaya Kalliopi lived in a tiny house they had purchased not far from our house, after moving to Tucson, Arizona to be closer to their children and grandchildren. We visited them every Sunday.

While my mother, aunts and uncles washed and dried the luncheon dishes, yiayia would begin the storytelling with her grandchildren at her feet. Sometimes gruesome tales of torture and subjugation followed. These were stories handed down to her by oral tradition from her grandmother Kalliopi who had lived through the final horrific days of the Ottoman occupation on the island of Crete. She closed these stories by telling us how young Greek women would fling themselves off the high cliffs surrounding Hania, her hometown, rather than be taken into the harems by the occupiers. My mother and aunt would come in at this point and tell her to stop frightening us. When they left, yiayia would close with the mantra that had been taught to her as a child, "We (Cretans and Greeks) would rather live an hour free than imprisoned like a bird."

Homer's Odyssey was also part of her storytelling repertoire. Her description of Odysseus and his men donning sheep's skins to fool the blinded cyclops into thinking they were sheep so that he would let them pass out of the cave into freedom was my favorite part. It wasn't until eight years later, as a sophomore sitting in a humanities class at the university, that I realized my illiterate grandmother knew Homer's tale by heart. She knew every part, even the nuances were spot on. Through no fault of her own she had not been schooled outside of the home. Her birth in 1897, in the tiny hamlet of Hania, Crete, and the fact that she was a female made formal schooling an impossibility. Her family struggled with poverty, as did most of the population following the end of the occupation. They did not complain, though. Their oppressors were now gone.

In 1912, at the age of fifteen, my grandmother and her brothers Andreas and Manos, left Hania for the mainland, where they would board a ship bound for

America. Four years later, while living with her sister and brothers in Akron, Ohio a pretty, young Kalliopi met a handsome, Greek man named Haralambos. He had come to woo her sister, Sophia, when he spotted Kalliopi. According to my mother, Kalliopi had been given the task of taking a towel to Haralmbos while he was shaving after an overnight stay. He tried to kiss her; she slugged him; and they fell in love. Papu loved her dearly.

Their love continued to grow throughout their marriage. Yiayia was a strong woman, who bore five children at home with the help of a midwife or experienced relative. During the births, my grandfather would take the other children to the movies, an unheard of extravagance for the immigrant father. When they returned, yiayia was up and mopping the afterbirth from the kitchen floor. She carried this strength of character into other areas of her dealings with papu. On nights when he would stay out late with his buddies playing cards and drinking the obligatory Ouzo shots, yiayia would be ready. After she heated up the stove, she removed all the chairs from the kitchen. Then she went to bed. Papu would come in the back door as quietly as he could. He needed to remove his shoes before proceeding through the rest of the house. The place for that was the kitchen. Unlucky for him that the Ouzo clouded his judgement and sight apparently.

My grandmother knew the exact moment that happened; the exact moment he sat on the open stove door. He'd remember the experience for a while, but then the boys would ask him out again. And once again, yiayia would remove the kitchen chairs after heating up the stove.

During prohibition years in the 1920s, when her children were small, yiayia personally frisked every male relative or friend who came to the house for a gathering. She then took the collection of guns to a secret place in the basement; usually under the olives collected for brining. Only when the men were out the door did they get their weapons back. My mother, being the oldest, knew exactly where the guns were; however, having been designated a guard by my grandmother and promised a trip with her on the streetcar when she next went to market, my mother kept her silence. Yiayia was true to her word and took my mother with her on the next shopping trip. They would stop for a jelly donut and coffee along the way. It was one of the rare times my mother had yiayia all to herself.

Papu was devastated by yiayia's death, as were her children. Although I was only eleven, I also took it hard. I was the one who would lead her from the bathroom to the sofa when we visited. I watched her comb her hair and braid it perfectly without benefit of sight. Her stories have stayed with me all my life. I am now a yiayia and realize what joy she knew when we sat at her feet and listened to her recitations. My yiayia stories are not as high brow as hers were. Mine are the adventures of my Shih Tzu Zorbas. However, I try to tell them with the same enthusiasm as yiayia did when describing how Odysseus fooled the cyclops.

My ancestral ties to yiayia's Cretan roots run deep. During a visit with my aunt Sophia to Hania in 1997, we had a chance to reconnect with our relatives. Many of them were named Pavlos or Paul, my great-grandfather's name. Many also had the same sandy hair and gray/green eyes. That one of my Bright Friends shared these characteristics is probably a coincidence. Probably. However, my aunt Sophia, shortly before her death, told me a secret. She had been visited by an 'angel' surrounded by bright light as a child. She never told anyone else this. She wasn't supposed to. I've kept her secret, until now.

DARKEST LIGHT

Her hands were soft
upon my face
her hands felt eyes and hair
Her hands were thorough
searching, seeking
for her eyes no more were there

My grandmother had cried great tears
great tears when sons were taken
to fight strange wars
kill and kill more
her soul was mightily shaken

She'd always said that was the way
she lost her sight so soon
Before late years
from many tears
from fears, and wars and doom

Her hands were soft
yet strong and safe
I still can feel them now
And how I wish to see
her face that shone with
love for me

I have those years
she spoke of tears
that doomed her sight forever
She gave me light
in darkest night
and told me fear not ever

I bear her name- Kalliopi
She was my pride and joy
Taken too soon
from tears of doom
My light in darkest night

CRETAN WOMEN

Blood had soaked the mountains
and made the brown dirt red
Still soldiers crawled
among their friends
Who now lay cold and dead

When nightfall came at last
the soldiers stopped to eat
Too busy with their victuals
they didn't hear the feet
of Cretan women
slowly, softly
coming towards their camp
Picking up the weapons
which from fresh blood still were damp

Soon the battle started
with different gun-hard eyes
The eyes of Cretan women
whose men or sons had died

And so that last fought battle
the one we know in depth
Where the Cretan women
picked up arms

and fought until their death
Their battle cry could far be heard
they shouted every word
"We'd rather live an hour free
than imprisoned like a bird"

And so the legend of that fight
in 1941
When the weary Allied soldiers
thought their victory was none
Had not predicted rightly
the Cretan woman's soul
For without an hour of freedom
no Cretan's ever whole

"Where Am I?"

I am cold and naked.
Where are my clothes?
We all are walking silently through the cold corridors.
Is this my high school?
The other adolescents look familiar.
I'm not holding my books. Where are my books?
One by one we each enter our designated rooms. The walls melt open to let us pass.
A message is sent to my mind; you are finished, you may go home.
I'm falling weightlessly through darkness.
I'm back home, lying paralyzed in bed.
Another message is sent; sleep now sleep now sleep...

‘Mother Finally Accepts What She Cannot Change’

I continued to be a challenge to my mother as I passed puberty and entered junior high school. I did well in school, and although I’m not a math wiz, I was put in an elevated math class. We were given ‘different’ mathematical puzzles to work out for homework. A fancy lead pencil was the prize for whoever solved the puzzle. One time the puzzle involved arranging numbers in a logical order. The students who figured it out had arranged them from lowest value to highest value. I raised my hand. “Miss Milne,” I said. “There’s another way that’s right as well.”

Miss Milne came over to my desk. She looked at my number order. Then she had me go up to the board and show the others. I got the pencil and a nod of approval from her, which was really something because Miss Milne was very economical in her praise of us. What she didn’t know was that I had been given the same type of puzzles by my Bright Friends when we were in the little classroom.

Mother and father often sat with me while we tried to work out the answers. One night the problem involved 3 cannibals and 3 explorers who had to cross a river. The sticky wick was that their canoe only held

3 people, and if one explorer was left with 2 cannibals during the crossing, the cannibals would eat him or her before reaching the other side. I can't remember if we solved it, but mother was determined to get the explorers to the other side in one piece.

Thankfully, I wasn't dragged around to revival tents or to the nuns or rabbi anymore. Something else had occurred to mother. She began reading about reincarnation and past lives.

"Do you remember anything about ancient Egypt?" she asked me one morning before I left for school.

"What?" I said. She was staring at me intently.

"What about ancient Greece? Any memories there?"

"I'm late mom," I hurried out the door before she went further with this new obsession.

Things changed when I began high school and started dating at age 15. My first boyfriend was a football player named Bob. He was one year older than I was and rode a motorcycle which added to his appeal. He was big and scruffy and had lovely hazel eyes. Best of all, he was crazy about me. We were only able to attend football games or other sport activities, go to school dances and approved parties.

After a month of our 'seeing' each other, mother asked Bob if he would like to come to lunch one Saturday. I was shocked. Bob was delighted. He arrived on time, and mother set a virtual Greek feast before him.

"More grape leaves Bob? Or Greek potatoes?" She couldn't do enough for him it seemed. However, just as Bob was chewing the last luscious potato wedge, mother sat across from him and shook her head sadly.

"I don't know what I'm going to do?" she lamented.

"What's the matter?" Bob wondered...right on cue.

"My friend is going to be so mad at me." Mother sounded desperate.

"Why?" Bob wondered as he continued to eat whatever she was putting on his plate.

Suddenly, in a shaking voice mother explained that her friend lived on the outskirts of town and had an olive grove. The trees were heavy with ripe olives, and mother had promised she and dad would help harvest them. Only now, according to mother, my father was covering for a sick cook at their restaurant. What was she to do?

"I can help." And that was all it took to draft Bob into mother's service. She hauled him away from the table so that he could help put the ladder in the car. Mother grabbed a sheet and me and we were off. I knew there was no friend on the outskirts of town. The olive groves belonged to a local rancher. Mother took Bob deep into the fragrant trees and had him climb up one while she spread out the sheet below. I was to stand where he could see me for encouragement. Bob fell out of the tree once, but mother made him go back up. When she was satisfied with the number of raw olives his shaking efforts had produced, mother let him come down. He was dizzy, and I was mortified. After Bob and I stopped going out, mother sized up every new guy for enlistment in future schemes.

At least she had stopped asking me about past lives.

One day the school nurse called.

"Karen might have appendicitis. You must take her to the doctor immediately."

A blood test and physical examination were positive for possible appendicitis, and I was hurried to St. Mary's hospital for surgery. I was seventeen, and mother somehow believed the doctor just wanted to make money on unnecessary surgery. After all no one in her family ever had a weak appendix. If I did have appendicitis, it was from dad's side. She stopped complaining when the doctor explained what he had found. My appendix was removed, not because it was infected and about to rupture, but because my right ovary had somehow 'moved' and was crowding it to a point where it had become irritated. With the appendix out of the way, things should return to normal the doctor reassured my parents. Three decades later, my right ovary would rupture from internal damage and require immediate surgery in New York. Back in Tucson in 1963, the doctor had a question for my parents.

"Has Karen had any surgical procedures on her ovaries?" He hesitantly asked. My mother was so offended she stormed off without dignifying his inquiry with an answer. I could have answered, but I was sworn to secrecy. From somewhere far off, a message was sent.

'Sleep, just sleep.'

"Jumping Through Time"

I was in a chemistry class at Tucson High School on the afternoon of November 22, 1963. The Vice-Principal came and asked our teacher Mr. Warren if he could have a word with him in the hall. After instructing us to continue with our experiments, Mr. Warren stepped outside. My partner Bill and I were lighting the Bunsen burner at our work station when he returned to the classroom. I will never forget his face. He was pale and appeared stunned. In a soft, somber voice he told us to gather our belongings and proceed to the cafeteria, where we would be dismissed for the day. There would be no school tomorrow either.

"President Kennedy has been assassinated," were his final words to us.

In stoney silence, we all gathered in the cafeteria. A television played the now infamous parade tape over and over. We watched the President fall into his wife, Jaqueline's, lap after being shot in the back of the head. We watched as the now widowed Mrs. Kennedy crawled over the trunk of the car towards the secret service agents walking behind the slow-moving car. We watched as an ambulance sped through the streets of Dallas in vain. Our president was already dead. Mrs. Kennedy's pink suit, soaked in blood, was a testament to the sacrifice her young husband had made in service to his country. My eyes filled with tears, and I couldn't watch anymore. I somehow found my sister, who was a senior to my sophomore status, and we walked home. Neither one of us said a word.

In church the following Sunday, President Kennedy was eulogized. I struggled to contain my tears as I sang memorial songs with other members of the choir. Once the service was over, I made my way to the ladies' room where my tears could flow freely.

"What's the matter?" my mother asked. "Did something upset you, Karen?"

"Yeah mom. I was alright until we sang "Amazing Grace", I explained.

"No, something else is wrong,"

She was right. I couldn't tell her that for the past several months, I had 'seen' President Kennedy's assassination in my mind. The 'visions' would occur in the twilight time just before I fell into a deep sleep. President Kennedy would be standing before a waving crowd, at a podium preparing to give a speech. Shots would ring out, and the next image I had was of him collapsing to the ground with blood pouring out of his head.

I suspected my Bright Friends were somehow responsible for these 'visions'; either they wanted me to recognize this newfound ability or it was a secondary 'gain', a collateral benefit of sorts resulting from our time together. I didn't allow myself to think about my premonitions. For a while, there were no more visions or pictures of anything disturbing intruding upon my subconscious mind prior to my falling asleep. That was going to change.

A short while later, I realized another vision was popping up during pre-sleep twilight. I saw a male relative, or someone I was close to, die a violent death, again by a bullet. The only person I could think of was my first cousin, who was flying a mission in Viet Nam. He was my Aunt Sophia's son, and we had been raised as brother and sister. Once again, I tried not to let the images enter my subconscious mind, to no avail. They stayed with me for two months, And then...

"Karen, it's mom," Mother was calling from the restaurant. It was after school, and I was doing homework.

"I'm going to pick you up, and then we are driving to Aunt Sarah's house. Uncle Eddie has committed suicide with a rifle." Uncle Eddie and Aunt Sarah were not our blood relatives. My father had baptized their oldest son, and in our church the godparent tie was as strong as any blood connection was.

This second 'actualization' of my visions made me realize this was not a fluke. I had become prescient whether I wanted to be or not. I shuddered to think what I would see next.

I didn't have to wait long.

Six months later, I was involved in a community theater production of a play by George Bernard Shaw. I had a small role, and my rehearsal schedule wasn't heavy. I could fit it in around my schooling and part-time job. By the time my head hit the pillow each night, I was more than ready to go to sleep. My exhaustion didn't prevent visions from entering my mind before surrendering to a deep sleep. What I saw this time was disturbing. On opening night of the play, a few weeks away, I would be wearing a cast on my left arm, and the arm would be supported by a sling.

I cased bookstores around town looking for information on premonitions; perhaps I could make them stop. I found nothing, and the days flew by. At night, no matter how long I stayed up reading or watching television, the images would flood my mind; my left arm was in a cast and sling on opening night. Soon it was the day of our dress rehearsal. As I would be at the theatre for several hours that night, I put a pork chop on to cook while I made some salad. I forgot to reduce the heat under the frying pan and with wet hands from washing the lettuce, I picked up the pan to move it. That's when it happened. My wet right hand fumbled with the handle of the frying pan and before I knew it hot grease had splattered all over the veins on the inside of my left wrist. Blood was pouring out of the damaged vessels opened by the second degree burn. At the emergency room, my entire left forearm was placed in a protective cast, and then in a sling after it was treated with local antibiotics. In addition, I was given some IV antibiotics, as well as oral ones to take for the next few weeks. My arm would be in the cast and sling for several weeks.

Did I intentionally injure my arm in a self-fulfilling prophecy attempt? Another prescient episode would convince me finally that something else was involved. Although there had been numerous premonitions that eerily hit the mark over the next two years, it wasn't until I was nineteen years old and a student at the University of Arizona that something occurred that was beyond simple coincidence.

"I have to go to papu's and spend the night," I abruptly announced to my mother one afternoon.

"What?" Although mother had grown more comfortable with my 'uniqueness', she never really relaxed totally.

"Why do you have to go?" Papu lived a few blocks away, and although he was a little frail, he was able to manage living on his own.

"I don't know, I just have to go tonight," I explained, packing an overnight bag.

"Well, I don't know what this is about, but I guess you'll tell me when you're ready." To her credit, mother trusted my instincts. I didn't tell her that it felt like a hand was on my back literally pushing me towards my grandfather's tiny three room home. I couldn't walk over there fast enough.

The next morning, I was in the little kitchen preparing breakfast when papu shuffled in. He did not greet me as he usually did. Instead, he went over to the shelf that held a bottle of Ouzo. He unscrewed the cap and drank some directly from the bottle. Then he turned around and in that instance I saw his face. One side of his mouth was paralyzed, as were the muscles around the eye above it. He was leaning unsteadily towards that side as he shuffled toward me, saying..."Kalliopi..." in a weak voice.

I took him to the living room and made the sofa into a bed for him. On my way to the phone, he began to cry. I saw that he had soiled the sheets with feces. I cleaned him up and brought him juice.

"Einae endaxi Papu." I reassured him in Greek that it was okay, and that I was going to call a doctor. I first called my mother, who brought the doctor right over. Papu had suffered a stroke; it may not have been the first one in the past few days. As the doctor was examining him, mother came over to me.

"How did you know?" she asked, with a measure of disbelief in her voice.

"I don't know. Maybe it was yiayia Kalliopi reaching across to me from the afterlife, imploring me to look after papu." At that moment that was as good an explanation as any for my mother. In fact, it was right up her alley, what with her recent obsession with past lives and the afterlife.

As comforting as it would have been for me to think that my grandmother, who had died eight years before, somehow alerted me to papu's impending stroke, I believed there was another possibility.

Perhaps my Bright Friends could manipulate time just as easily as they manipulated the molecules in a wall to 'melt' so that they could pass through. Whatever the reason was for my sudden 'gift', I wanted no part of it. Who would? Although I had been of help to my grandfather when he needed it, I also was frightened to realize the premonition of my arm being injured came true. I decided an intervention was necessary.

"Hello. Are you there?" I said to no one. I was standing in the middle of papu's tiny living room, all alone.

"Look, I appreciate the 'gift', I really do. Thanks a bunch. However, I really don't want it. I'm a faulted human; I have feet of clay. I want to be buried with prayers at the end of my life. At this rate, the best my relatives will be able to do for me will be to put coins on my eyes, light me afire and send me across a river when I die. So can I return it, please? You don't have to answer me now. Think about it. Thanks anyway. Bye."

As I phased out of Part Two of my visitation years (ages 11-19) and into the final five years (ages 20-25), I had no idea how many future events in my life I would 'see'. This ability stayed with me after I left Tucson to move to New York City; in fact, it has been with me my whole life. I try not to see too far in advance now, as I'm almost 70 years of age. Being buried with prayers would be nice.

"Yes, I can correct this problem," Dr. Howzer, a plastic surgeon, said while he examined my breasts.

"Hmmn. This is odd," the doctor said mostly to himself.

"What is?" Mother was gifting the surgery to me as a birthday present. I would be nineteen soon, and she knew my right breast would never catch up to my left. For some reason it never developed past puberty.

"What's odd doctor?" mother repeated.

"There are some very fine scars present. If I didn't know better..."

Mother looked for the lines.

"My guess is breast tissue has been removed."

"Karen has never had surgery on her breasts. You're the first doctor she's visited." Mother scoffed.

That wasn't true, I thought sitting silently on the examining table.

And then came a familiar question.

"Are you sure Karen hasn't had surgery on her breast before?"

Again, I sat silent.

Again I could have answered the query.

Again, I kept my secret.

"We are entering white water, nothing seems right. We don't know where we are..."

(pilot of Flight 19 missing over 'the Bermuda Triangle,' 1962)

According to the US Navy, the triangle does not exist. (Wikipedia, 2016)

"The Dairy Farmer"

I once watched a dairy farmer help a cow deliver her calf. It happened while I was on a university field trip in 1969. The event was unplanned, however our insightful leader decided this was something we would never be privy to again. He was right. The other cows in the enclosure were interested in watching the calf literally being pulled by a chain from out of the mother. Some members of our group, females as well as males, became dizzy and were led outside for fresh air. I stayed; this was fascinating. The mother cow seemed to know the farmer was helping her, even though her head was immobilized in a steel harness. She had been in labor for twelve hours and the chances of a live birth were diminishing the longer the labor continued. Finally a calf covered in blood and amniotic fluid was birthed. The farmer took what looked like a large baster and sucked the mucous from the calf's nose and mouth. He then rubbed it vigorously with a towel and even shook it by its forelegs. I was getting alarmed, until the little cow finally took a breath on its own. It was a girl; she was perfect. Those of us who had stayed were crying. Some of the others came back in to see this miracle of life. After having been let out of her harness, the mother cow came over and licked her calf. She was butting it with her nose, in an attempt to make it stand up. We were allowed to wait until the baby stood on its wobbly legs. Soon it would begin nursing. The mother and baby knew what to do next. We all left them alone.

A symbiotic relationship existed between the farmer and the cows, it was explained to us. They co-existed in a world I had never seen before. The farmer made sure the cows were cared for: fed and grazed and treated by a vet when sick. They, in turn, gave him milk and more calves. There was no doubt as to who held the power; the farmer had final say on everything concerning the cows. Yet, without the cows' cooperation there would be no milk, no calves and his livelihood would falter. Dairy farmers, our group leader explained, had both respect and love for their herds. Each cow was important to them; they often referred to them as 'family members'; each birth was celebrated, each death was mourned. They were each a part of the other's equation; neither complete without the other. Of course, we had visited a rather small dairy farm on the outskirts of Tucson in 1969. Dairy farming was changing as new technology made the production of milk an enterprise rather than a family business. Still, there were farmers who refused to expand. Their cows were family, and they would have it no other way. I was grateful to have seen the birth of one such newest family member.

Almost six decades later, as I try to make sense of who my Bright Friends were; what our relationship was; and why they visited me...the image of the dairy farmer helping his cow birth her calf came to mind. I knew the following: my visitors loved me (us); they didn't speak our language but we still could communicate; they visited often and made sure all was well with me. Also, they considered me 'family'. Although I realize that my Bright Friends and I were related beyond a simple feeling, the dairy farmer analogy still fit in many ways. We were a part of their world, and they were a part of our world. A symbiotic relationship existed, though our society did not accept their existence in 1969, nor do we now.

Obviously, I am not a dairy farmer, nor a biologist nor any type of agricultural professional. I am a mother and grandmother. I do remember the birth of both my children. I did not have drugs and thank God everything went well. However, when I arrived at the hospital in labor the second time in July of 1980, the attending physician told me not to push as the doctor was stuck on the Long Island Expressway. I couldn't believe she told me that. I had no intention of not pushing. Actually, at the point she said this the baby was in control and making her way out. Fortunately, the doctor arrived in time for the final moments. I was grateful for the help, but I somehow felt the baby and I might have been able to manage on our own, if we had to. Yiayia Kalliopi had, and she even got up to mop the kitchen floor afterward. I am forever grateful for the miracle of my children and grandchildren. They have been my greatest joy in life, and I will continue to thank God until my dying day for their blessings.

Dairy farmers, cattle ranchers and sheep herders are not the only members of a species that raise their food or food providers. Ants raise colonies of aphids as a food source, termites cultivate fungi to eat, and damselfish tend algae gardens to the point where they weed out whatever's inedible and spit it out in designated garbage dumps. Apparently, human domestication of animals and vegetation as food sources is relatively new compared to when other lifeforms on earth began their farming efforts. As usual, we (humans) like to think we 'invented' farming techniques. If we didn't invent them, we have improved them. However we want to delude ourselves, nature trumps us. We have blinders on. We like to think are masters of the universe. We want to believe there are no visitors in UFOs able to 'control' us. I understand how unsettling this is. But denying it doesn't make it go away. Perhaps we have to think in these terms to survive. I don't know.

I do know that all lifeforms on earth exist in relation to one another. I was very sick the fall prior to a recent Christmas visit with my son and his family on the west coast. I couldn't shake a stubborn bronchitis. A doctor visit verified my lungs were finally clear, and I left for the holiday journey. We were wrong. One day after my arrival, I succumbed to yet another, more aggressive bronchial attack. This time, upon my return, I was given a much stronger antibiotic. It was so strong I became sick each time I took it. A battle was being waged between the germs that wanted to live and my immune system. Thankfully, the antibiotic helped me win the battle. Without it, I am certain the outcome would have been horribly different.

Whoever our visitors are, they have been a part of our world since our first appearance on the planet. It was communicated to me by my Bright Friends that we, their species and humans, are related; we are family. One group of visitors looked just like us, save for the brilliant light that often surrounded them. I may never discover the answers I seek as to where they are from and what their exact intent toward us is. During the final years of those first twenty-five, the mountain visit years, information was communicated to me that would help me understand the who and why of it all.

Life is full of mysteries. If I tried to unravel each one as I journey through, I might never make headway. Some are worth unravelling; others may not be. In retrospect I should have told my mother that I truly had been Cleopatra, Queen of the Nile and that Marc Antony had been a 'hunk'.

"Betty and Barney Hill's Experience and Me"

On September 19, 1961, in the White Mountains of New Hampshire, Betty and Barney Hill had an experience with a UFO and alien visitors. They were traumatized to the extreme, and afterwards both had terrifying dreams reliving what had occurred. Seeking help for the post-traumatic stress, they began rigorous testing and hypnosis sessions with a noted psychiatrist. A book, "The Interrupted Journey" by John G. Fuller published in 1966 brought their story to a fascinated, yet disbelieving, public. Their lives were forever altered, not so much by the actual experience, but because the Hills remembered much of what had happened, sought psychiatric help and unwittingly became poster children for a newly formed club of sorts: those who claim to have been abducted.

I read John Fuller's book when it was first published. In 1966, I was 19 years of age living with my grandfather, attending the University of Arizona and working two jobs after school. The last thing I needed was to be associated with what mainstream society labeled a 'lunatic fringe' of individuals believing in UFOs and little gray men with horrific eyes. I wasn't ready to come forward and society wasn't ready to accept on any level the possibility that we were under alien surveillance. We have come a long way since then, both society and me personally. At least now UFOs and aliens are being openly discussed. There are television programs entirely dedicated to connecting ancient archeological mysteries with the possibility that aliens were responsible, in part or altogether.

It troubled me that the Hills had been terrified by their experiences. It occurred to me that because they hadn't been followed since birth, as I had been, they didn't get to know their visitors personally. It also occurred to me that the ones that visited Betty and Barney, were not exactly the same as the ones that visited me. My Bright Friends had communicated to me that although their group was well-intentioned, some others who visited earth were not. In my final five years of these first twenty-five (from 20-25), I would receive information during mountain visits about these 'others'. My visitors also communicated that the good ones were more powerful than the others. It seemed to be the universal conflict of good versus evil. It became obvious to me that a vast and complicated system of visitations had been occurring since we, humans, arrived on the planet; whether we want to believe it or not. I am not saying the visitors are God; far from it. Just as we now manipulate genetics and eugenics, they did so eons ago, perhaps to cultivate a hybrid race capable of colonization on earth for economic reasons. Whatever the genesis, the reality in 1961, when the Hills were abducted, was that this activity had been going on a very long time; long enough for corruption to enter the equation.

From the drawings and descriptions of the little men that visited the Hills, it was obvious none of them resembled humans. The Hills did not mention the bright light that usually accompanied a visit. Perhaps the trauma blocked their memory. My messenger verified that 'people' usually didn't remember; and they (my visitors) didn't know why I was.

Another puzzling aspect of the Hills' experience, was that Betty described books and maps, in the forms that exist on earth today, that were used by the aliens. No maps or books were present, ever, in a printed form on any of the ships I visited during those first 25 years. The toys and learning equipment in the little blue classroom/playroom were technically more advanced than anything available on earth at the time (circa 1950). I was given plastic figures of human men, women and children and also figures of my visitors as they taught me about our relationship and connection. Betty Hill related that she had wanted to take one of the books with her. Again, this seems so different than any of my experiences. I can only conclude that the Hills were not 'in for life' as I was. They might have been visited more than once, however. Being an interracial couple, somewhat unique at that time, they presented an interesting human couple for study and sample taking (harvesting).

In the book it is also explained that the aliens were confused when Barney's false teeth came out of his mouth during the examination. This validates, for me, the theory that these visitors were unauthorized pirate types, who had no background in human anatomy. Had they been scientists, as some of mine were, they would have known about human dental practices, including false teeth. In addition, Betty was about fifty when she was visited and quite possibly past her child bearing years. Yet, the aliens wanted to see if she was pregnant, despite Betty's explanation that she was not. The level of interaction alone is extremely divergent from what occurred during my visits; and I knew my Bright Friends. However, I wholly believe that the Hills were visited, but by a splinter group that was unauthorized to do so. Regrettably, many such groups comprise part of the UFOs visiting earth and abducting study subjects. Their main purpose is not to further their knowledge of our species, but to harvest whatever they can in human DNA for sale on a galactic black market.

If we keep denying the existence of UFOs and aliens, we are complicit in encouraging ruthless, ill intentioned, self-serving pirates to do what they want to us without regard for our ultimate well-being. My Bright Friends were not a part of this group. Someday the distinction between who's authorized to visit earth and us and whose not, will be regulated by both well-intentioned aliens and their human counterparts on earth. However, this will only happen if we grow up, throw out our egos and recognize that UFOs and aliens are here to stay and are an integral part of our history and future. It's about time.

<u>"Curiouser and Curiouser!"</u>

-Lewis Carroll, Alice in Wonderland

"Saying Goodbye Again...For A Little While"

I stopped eating and took a day off from work. Something happened the night before; what was it? He had come to see me again, the Bright Friend who always watched over me. They couldn't contact me for a while; but, I would see them again. It was communicated that the next group of visits would change dramatically. I was not to be afraid. If I needed him, he would make sure I was alright. He would be right behind me, with his hand on my back.

In addition to being upset about the impending separation, I was recovering from a very odd situation. For the past seven months I had missed my period. No doctor could discover the cause. They told me I might be pregnant. Since I was still a virgin, I knew this was impossible. One month later, I awoke in a sea of blood. My period had come back in a flood. I threw out the bloody sheets in the event mother questioned me about them. That was all I needed. I slowly recovered. Four years later, this situation would repeat itself. I would find myself without a period, during a time I had not been with anyone for months. Only decades later did I realize that perhaps I had been carrying embryos; ones I was not destined to keep. My body type was a long-waisted one. Even when I was 29 years old and 7 months pregnant with my first child, people couldn't always tell I was carrying a baby.

If I had been pregnant, the embryos wouldn't have been all human. Certainly not the first one, when I was 19 and a virgin. Even at 23 years of age, and in between relationships, I had always been careful. It is difficult to think about these past events being a mother and grandmother. I can only repeat that it seemed alright; I was a part of something that would benefit our world and their world; I trusted and loved them. And in the end, what choice did I have? I had never known a time they weren't in my life.

The period of separation passed slowly. I felt as if something was missing from my life. I couldn't always put it in quantifiable terms, but the absence was palpable. I did not attend the university that semester. Mother was in a quandary. Once again she searched for answers. Was I on drugs? Had someone been mean to me? She was relentless in her maternal instinct to protect me. Whatever or whoever was causing her usually upbeat daughter to turn quiet and listless would be found out by her. I used to resent this quality in her back in those days. I now realize she was just being what she thought was a good mother. If I could only turn back the clock and tell her the real reason I was melancholy; but, at least for now, we do not have that luxury.

After I turned twenty, and apparently phased out

of the temporary separation period, things returned to normal. I knew they were back in my life. What I didn't know was that they were easing my transition into one of the more frightening visitation experiences in my history of being abducted. True to his word, my familiar Bright Friend reassured me when I would get frightened. As frightening as this period was, it was critical to what I am now doing. I began to put some of it together back then, but I would have to live a lifetime to put it all together. However, back in 1967 I went back to the university to complete my degree in education. I had a new boyfriend and life was good.

Part Three

The Mountain Years

(ages 20-25)

"Where were you yesterday afternoon?" my mother asked during our regular Monday chat.

"I was busy, mom."

"What's wrong? You sound congested. Are you getting sick?"

"I'm just tired."

"So where were you yesterday? Some mystery man?" Mother was determined I would get married before turning into an old maid past the age of 25. I was 23 and clearly in the danger zone.

"No mystery man." My voice was fading fast.

"Make some of that Greek tea I gave you. Put a spoon of honey in it."

"You do know my friends all think it's marijuana." I loved teasing her.

"I don't think that's funny. So, where were you, Karen?" She wasn't going to drop the question.

"I went for a ride in the desert."

"Why? What's the draw out there, and please do not tell me it's the scenery again!"

"I just like driving in the desert on Sunday afternoons. It's pleasant."

"It's nuts, that's what it is. You know I can find out where you go. I have friends all over town."

"I know mom. The ones that told you Bruce and I were getting engaged because we looked in a jewelry store window." Bruce was an anthropology student at the university working towards a masters degree and my current boyfriend. Mother did not approve of Bruce, who chain-smoked Camel cigarettes.

"Yes, those friends. If you do ever get engaged to Bruce, I'm giving him money to buy another jacket. The one he has, the only one he has, smells to high heaven of smoke."

"Great."

"So, where were…"

"Mom, I have to grade papers. Say hi to dad. I'll call you tomorrow."

I couldn't have explained it even if I wanted to. How could I? There were no words in my vocabulary that would describe what happened during the three hours that went missing every Sunday I took a desert ride. Still, I was at peace with it. It was all part of my relationship with my Bright Friends. It was okay. It was right.

"Escaping the Hospital"

My friend Gil was driving; he was taking me to the hospital. I had been deathly ill for two weeks, in the infirmary at the university. The doctors there were baffled. They couldn't find a cause for my illness; moreover complicated blood test results were beyond their laboratory capabilities to analyze. The doctor treating me advised my parents that I needed to be in a fully equipped hospital. I was 20 and had just started back as a second semester sophomore; fortunately spring break was a day away. My friend Gil drove me to the Tucson Medical Center, the same hospital I had been born in.

They did every test in the book on me, never telling me what they were looking for. I couldn't believe I had any blood left, so much had been taken. Groups of interns came into my room and examined me. When our priest came and gave me last rites, I had no alternative. I knew exactly what to do.

I waited until night; the hospital staff thinned out for the graveyard shift. I got out of bed and tiptoed out of the room. My feet were bare intentionally; if the nurses saw my slippers they might think I was in the bathroom. I had closed the door and left the water in the sink run slightly to buy time for my escape.

I stood in a darkened corner, then quickly followed

one of the nurses leaving for the night, in order not to trip the exit alarm. She didn't hear my bare feet on the slate far behind her. Never once did it cross my mind how dangerous my bare feet were outside. Anyone living in the desert knows that snakes, scorpions, gila monsters and other poisonous citizens of the sand patrol at night, after the blazing sun sets. This was not my main concern. I had to contact my 'friends'.

"Hello," I said searching the velvet sky. "Are you there? I'm in trouble. Please help me."

The next thing I remember, I was walking back toward the hospital. Two orderlies were frantically searching the grounds when one spotted me.

"We found her!" They shouted.

"Bring a blanket," another ordered. "She's freezing and may be in shock."

"I'm not in shock." I calmly said.

Once inside, the attending physician stood by my bed.

"Where were you? Three hours has passed. And how did you get out without tripping the alarm?" the doctor asked, clearly disturbed at the patient who escaped during his watch.

"I just felt like taking a walk in the desert." I truthfully answered. The urge to go outside began while I was still in my hospital room, upset at the last rites that were given me.

"Without shoes? In your condition?" the doctor continued.

"And just what condition is that?" I demanded. "You've told me nothing, and the next thing I know my priest is preparing for my funeral. What's wrong with me."

"You're bloodwork is highly unusual." The doctor said studying my chart.

"We're all unique. I'll tell you everything if you take one more blood test right now. And rush the results. Deal?"

"A blood test?"

"Yes, right now...and rush the results." I knew my Bright Friends had fixed me; what I didn't know was how long the fix would stick.

I stayed awake until the doctor came back several hours later.

"You seemed to have experienced a remarkable recovery." He said looking at the paper in his hands.

"Great. Then I can go home?" I wasn't in the mood to make any more deals.

"You said you'd explain everything," he reminded me.

"Okay. You know those Reeses monkeys that you used to experiment on in medical school? I'm like them, only a human test subject. I was involved in a secret study at the university. It involved reactions to new medications. I was paid to participate. It's super secret and if you say anything, I'll deny ever telling you that."

I was counting on his young doctor's paranoia to kick in. Although, in truth I was a test subject; just not on earth. He took a moment to consider. I was praying he wouldn't call the psychiatric resident. He didn't.

"I'll prepare your release form immediately. You can go home now or in the morning." The young intern said.

I picked up the phone.

"Gil, can you come and get me? They're kicking me out."

Perhaps my blood irregularities were a byproduct of my abductions; perhaps not. I was attending classes, working two jobs, going to choir practice and taking drives in the desert on weekends. And amazingly, despite my bare feet, not a mark was on them when I returned. I know, because the young doctor had examined them. He knew something was very odd; he didn't know what. I had lived with not knowing the whys and the hows for the past twenty years. Welcome to my world.

"The Moose Calf"

I saw a program about a baby moose calf as it was followed, with its mom, through a national preserve in Vancouver. Recent deaths of moose calves were why they were being tracked and followed through their first year of life. Researchers following the calf had to stay hidden and not interfere in the interactions between the calf and the mother. However, the calf did have to be 'collared' so that the researchers could follow it. Both the mother and her baby were sedated slightly, and the calf had a hood put over its head to cover its eyes while the researchers collared her. The hood was removed once the procedure was over.

The tricky part came when the calf and mother were reunited. Would she detect a human interference and abandon the calf to fend for itself and surely die? Fortunately, in this instance the mother accepted her calf back and off they went through the preserve.

I know how the calf felt.

When I was very young, during the early years of my visitations, my eyes would be covered as we approached the ships to board. I would peek out from under the protective hand of my Bright Friend and look anyway.

Warding off possible extinction of the Vancouver

moose species was the reason the researchers were studying the mother cow and her calf.

Is the human race in danger of extinction?

Habitat destruction is the main reason a species will die out. If their environment becomes hostile to their survival, the species is doomed.

We know we are hurting our environment with many technological advancements. The question is 'can we stop?'

I believe my Bright Friends were conducting a study exactly like the one the researchers following the baby moose calf were conducting. During the second part of my visitations, the harvesting years, my ova were collected, were harvested. I know my visitors were benevolent. They were loving and kind and treated me like precious cargo.

Just the way the researchers treated the baby moose. They were over the moon about the calf. They thought the baby was just fabulous; they said so as they watched it frolic.

I used to frolic around the ships, to the delight of my 'researchers'.

Whether we want to accept it or not, we are one species in a vast universe of many lifeforms. My Bright Friends did the same things to me that we do to lifeforms we are attempting to help; to save. I realize how difficult it is for many to accept this. However, we do have one card to play. We are 'related to them; we are family.' The researchers were not related to the baby calf. If we can establish contact, benevolent contact, with these alien researchers then we will be able to stop the illegal poaching of human DNA, ova, sperm, etc. all over the planet. And we might just help stop our extinction.

"Inside the Pyramid"

An invisible hand was on my back, or in my mind, pushing me to take a ride in the desert. It was Sunday, and I had just had lunch with my parents upon returning from church. I wasn't student teaching nor scheduled to work at Sears. There was no choir practice for upcoming holiday programs. My afternoon was free; and that's when the urge would come, as regularly as a sunrise.

My mother raised her eyebrows when I told her I was leaving.

"You're going for a ride again?" she asked while washing the dishes.

"I'm just going out, mom." I was twenty-two years of age and didn't have to explain innocent behavior to my mother.

"Your father thinks you have a secret lover," she casually said.

"Well then I must hurry before he gets sunstroke standing under the sahuaro I'm to meet him at." And I left. I couldn't explain the urge to drive in the desert any more than I could explain who my Bright Friends really were.

I was on automatic pilot during the thirty minute drive. Traffic on South Sixth Ave. was very slow due to the twenty-five mile per hour speed restriction.

It wouldn't be until I was almost at Ajo Way that the restriction was lifted. I made a right turn at Ajo and drove due west. The road soon became unpaved; the year was 1969, and the city had yet to expand all the way to the foothills.

I recognized the area though there were no street markers anywhere and drove my little Volkswagen on a side road that led directly to where the foothill ended and the mountain began. Next, I turned off the car motor and checked the time. I was supposed to check the time. I believe my visitors wanted me to know what was happening. It had been planned since I showed promise during the early visits; I had been the 'smart monkey'. I also loved and trusted them; moreover, I understood them somehow.

I looked at my watch again. Three hours had passed. I didn't question why or how. I simply drove straight to my apartment and began grading student's papers. Everything was normal; everything was as it should be. I felt rested and calm, and a little happy; as if I had just visited with a loving relative. The rest of my Sunday ended normally. Friends joined me for dinner at a favorite Mexican restaurant. We stayed longer than planned, and I was exhausted by the time I got home. Falling asleep came easily.

Suddenly I awoke. Panic gripped me. I looked at the time; it was 3am. What a nightmare! I had been inside a clear sarcophagus in a vast pyramid, and I was not alone. Hundreds of others were in clear boxes with me. I couldn't speak or move, but I could breathe. The nightmare had seemed very real.

'Help me.' I thought the words. 'Put me out again, please'. I didn't like this at all.

Next, a muted swoosh accompanied me as I tumbled through a cylindrical passageway, unbelievably fast. Everything was dark around me, but I could feel the confines of the passageway as I sped through it. The next thing I knew I was in my bed, freezing cold and shaking.

'You weren't supposed to awaken.' I was thinking this, but I had not originated the thought.

I threw a coat over my pajamas and drove to my parent's house. I didn't want to sleep in my apartment that was certain.

"What are you doing here?" my mother asked in the morning, standing over the living room couch where I was sleeping.

"What time is it?" I asked, realizing I had left my clothes at my place.

"It's 6:30. Do you want breakfast?" Mother looked at me; she was concerned.

"Just coffee. I'm due at school by 8." I couldn't explain. I had not figured it out yet, and I was not about to worry my mother. This was my journey; a lonely journey, for now.

Driving to school that day, I remembered bits

of information. I knew somehow that information had been transferred to me during the three missing hours when I was at the mountain foothill. I knew I had been inside the mountain. I also knew I had been inside a clear sarcophagus of sorts. There were many others just like me. We were being fed information; information to help us. One of the messages concerned me far into the future; many decades later, I would write about my visitation experiences. I would have to experience many life events first, decades would pass.

Great. That didn't help me back in 1969. I had to trust my instincts, and I had to trust my Bright Friends. Someday it would fall into place. For now, I needed to finish out the semester of student teaching. I was scheduled to accompany some students on a trip to Greece the following year. Perhaps when I touched down on ancestral soil, everything would make sense. Jesus help me; Jesus make it so.

"Nasty Alien Pirates"

During the final five years, the mountain visitations, I was given information about those my visitors identified as 'the not well-intentioned ones'. It saddened my friends to inform me of them. My Bright Friends were kind and benevolent. Whatever they did to me was never for personal gain nor for entertainment; it was to help people become stronger and better. They are related to us; they are family. They were here before us, and they have an obligation to us. They also want us to be aware of their struggle to rid our planet of exploitation by the 'bad guys'.

In our great human population there are good individuals (well-intentioned) and not so good individuals (not well-intentioned). It is part of our human make-up. We are in a struggle against good and evil at some point in our lives; for some, like addicts, it is a daily struggle. For others, being ill-intentioned or negative may be just how they prefer to operate. For some it is driven by greed. The exploitation of others is as old as ancient Egypt. For the Egyptians to offer the Hebrew slaves money for their efforts would empower them. It would not have been economically feasible; the Hebrews had to remain subjugated and enslaved for Egypt to rise to splendor. In other words, they had to be exploited.

It is the same for my visitors; my Bright Friends. They are hundreds of thousands of years older than the human race. I saw two varieties of visitors: human looking ones and little blue/grey fellows. I'm sure there are many more varieties in their world and other worlds in distant galaxies. There will also be well-intentioned individuals within these groups, as well as not so well-intentioned ones. Their societies will be a mix of good and bad members, just like here on earth. It is the way of the universe: positive versus negative; good versus evil.

When I read about or see a television program about people being frightened and harassed by evil spirits or nasty ghosts, I believe they are really aliens exploiting us for fun and profit, illegally. Many times the people being troubled describe being paralyzed, just as I was on my returns from visits. At other times, people describe bright lights followed by dark figures that can materialize or disappear instantly. All these powers are within the technology of alien visitors. Here on earth, we watch reality television to vicariously see people treating other people badly; it's the sad truth. I believe an inter-galactic black market exists in their entertainment industry. It caters to an alien audience that gets off watching the humans flip out when harassed by the annoying and sometimes dangerous intruders. They, the alien pirates, scare the wits out of us. It must be a huge success and a real coup to pull off. The invading presence must identify itself if confronted by priests or exorcists; they try not to. If they do, they will be apprehended by their own species and dealt with severely.

These alien pirates on our planet also may be responsible for cattle and animal mutilations; for planes and ships disappearing in the Bermuda Triangle and possibly for crop circles (the least harmful of their exploits). Many decades after my mountain visits, where information about these alien nasties was transferred to me, I would try to tell one of my priests in New York about my Bright Friends. When my priest wanted to know if they were evil, I had to tell him no. My visitors were benevolent and kind. Somehow I was protected from the alien pirates. My messenger, the one who came to my room when I was very young, implied as much right before he left when he unconsciously sent me a message: "You are fortunate." I've tried to figure out what he meant all my life. Only now, sixty-five years later do I realize what he was communicating. Perhaps my Bright Friends knew I would write about this someday, and they protected me from abduction and exploitation by the other ones. I realize the cross over to religious history seems more than coincidental. However, I hold my religion separate and apart from science and certain events in the world. My religion is about hope, love and endurance. My intent is not to disavow any religion; I respect all religions.

If we continue to deny the fact that aliens have and still do visit our planet, we are empowering the ones who wish to exploit and harm us, the humans on the planet. If, however, we are one day able to acknowledge an alien presence as a reality and part of life on planet earth, then we are on our way to open communication with the 'good guys', the ones who have been struggling to protect us from the others. I know this day will come; perhaps not in my lifetime, but it will definitely arrive. The truth always comes out and good trumps evil.

"An Ancestral Journey"

I felt a hand on my back at times, leading me towards my path in life. Because I had experienced things my friends and family members hadn't, I decided to trust my instincts and go where I was directed. I was twenty-three and teaching school. My summers were free, and I decided to apply for a position as a chaperone to students visiting Greece; my years in Greek school were about to be put to the test. A position opened, and the following summer I would visit the land of my ancestors. I couldn't wait.

When the pilot announced we had touched down in Athens I felt electricity surge through me. This was the city my father had lived and worked in before coming to the United States. This was the land both my paternal and maternal grandparents had been born in. I was home in the best sense of the word. Our group was scheduled to visit Sparta, which was very near to Tripoli the largest town adjacent to the village of Tziba, my father's birthplace. I took a day off to visit remaining relatives. They were quite surprised at a visit by Vasily's daughter. A thea, or aunt, made hilopites, a lovely light noodle, she mixed with broth. Figs, fruit, cheese and homemade bread were set before me. We ate outside, with the surrounding mountains providing unforgettable scenery. Our goodbyes were filled with promises of a return trip by me. My life would change dramatically in the next few years. I had no idea I would return to Greece in four short years. The hand on my back was steadier and stronger than ever.

After touring the mainland, we boarded a cruise ship for the islands. Crete was on the itinerary, of course, as it is the largest of the Greek islands. I didn't make it to my grandmother Kalliopi's village of Hania on this journey, but I would return in twenty-five years with my aunt Sophia for an extended visit. As I toured Minoan palaces, the wind whistled through olive groves and I could almost hear Homer's words. From whom had my grandmother heard the epic tales of the Iliad and the Odyssey? How had their integrity held over millenniums by oral history alone? My grandmother had not read Homer's great works in a book; she couldn't read. By sharing this oral history with her grandchildren, my yiayia Kalliopi transferred more than Homer's epics; she transferred the spirit of the people who had kept the tales alive.

The days and nights of my journey flew quickly by, and soon it was time to return to my desert land. My father hoped I would come home with a husband; mother wanted me to come home and decide that the Greek tomato farmer who lived across the border in Mexico and who had been pursuing me to mother's delight with bushels of tomatoes was the one.

Neither got their wish. Events on this journey would shape my future decisions in ways none of us had ever expected. Soon, I would be living two thousand, I would be living two thousand miles from Tucson in New York City, embarking on a few decades of life that would not be shared with my Bright Friends. My heart was too full of promise and hope as I flew back from the land of my ancestors to worry about what that might be like. My ancestors had journeyed far from the only home they knew to begin fresh; it had been their destiny. My destiny was calling. It was a siren's song I could not ignore. The hand on my back pressed harder.

"Highway I-19"

While teaching Language Arts to young adolescents at Carson Jr. High School, I realized my degree in secondary education had not included early reading skills for students who had difficulty in this area. After completing course work in how to teach reading, I was offered a job with Continental School, a K-8 school that served the ranching and farming communities between Tucson and Nogales. I would be teaching migrant children, as well as the children of the ranchers and farmers. The challenge appealed to me, and I accepted the position. The year was 1972, and it would be my final year of living and teaching in Arizona.

In order to reach the tiny school, where many of the classrooms were trailers, I drove south on Highway I-19. From my apartment on Tenth Ave. and Highland in the center of town, the drive took almost an hour if I stayed within the speed limit. Once on the highway in the early morning hours, traffic was almost non-existent. In 1972 there were very few signs or structures on the roadsides. Only the road, the mountains, the sky and the desert surrounded me for most of the ride. For all intents and purposes, I was alone. Or at least I thought I was alone.

Out of habit I would check the time and my

odometer for milage once I entered I-19. My radio would be tuned to my favorite country western or soft rock station and a thermos of coffee sat in the passenger seat in case the monotony of the road made me sleepy. In truth, that almost never happened. More often than not, I would find myself twenty miles farther down the road than I was supposed to be; almost instantaneously. Even more curious was the odometer, only a few miles had registered from the time I started on the highway. When I tried to think about the twenty minutes needed to travel as far as I had, my mind was blank. I couldn't pull up the memory of passing any of the familiar terrain.

I never told anyone about this phenomenon. At the time, I didn't connect it to my Bright Friends. It was just another anomaly in my unusual life. Not until over forty years later would I realize what had really happened during the missing miles. It had been in my memory all along; I only had to lift the curtain to find it.

What really happened on Highway I-19?

My radio was the first indication that something was occurring; static replaced the songs. Next I was not in control of my car; in fact, my hands were still on the steering wheel but were frozen in place. Also, my feet couldn't change from the accelerator to the brake pedal. Something or someone else was 'driving' my car. And then, though still in my car, I was not on the road anymore. I was nowhere. I only felt this for a few unnerving minutes, which seemed much longer to me. Bright light surrounded me; I felt a shudder and then slowly I realized I was in my car again...on the highway...except I was twenty miles further down the road from where I was when this experience began. I did not see any of my Bright Friends during the experience, but I felt they were near me whenever this occurred. I am not a physics genius, but whatever happened on I-19 involved time and space manipulation (to me and my car by others).

Although it seemed as if I had been 'away' in the brilliant light for only a short time, body indicators told a different story. By the time I arrived at the school, areas of my skin were irritated. The marks resembled small rug burns, usually on my upper back. I finally realized skin had been scraped from these areas by some kind of instrument. Occasionally, although the massive nosebleeds of my early childhood had long since subsided, blood would begin to flow from my nose with no apparent cause. When my teaching colleagues expressed concern, I told them the bleeding was caused by a new allergy medication my doctor had given me. The final physical indicator was a ringing in my ears. Except for the scraped areas of skin, the nosebleeds and ringing in my ears stopped after an hour or so. Thankfully, my colleagues did not see the marks on my back; those would have been difficult to explain away.

Even if I wanted to, how would I have explained what was happening to me? In 1972, although UFO sightings in Arizona were not unusual, the subject of alien abductions was not encouraged. Arizona was a very conservative state, in all ways back in those days. I would have been labeled 'eccentric' at best; possibly even crazy. My teaching job would have been jeopardized, as well as my standing in my church and community. As the bright messenger had communicated to me many years before, 'it would be better if you did not tell anyone about the visits.' So I didn't.

"The Cliff Hanger"

During those final five years of visitations, my life was changing rapidly. I graduated from college and began teaching. In order to help my students better, I went back to the University of Arizona for graduate work in education. My teaching salary was modest, so I took on waitressing one night a week at the restaurant of a family friend. In addition, I signed with a modeling agency and did radio, television and print ads in my free time. The agency, Fossi's, served local merchants. I sold hay and feed for ranchers on the radio, appeared in print dry cleaning ads for a family-owned dry cleaners and one time spent an entire day eating Lay's potato chips for a television ad. I no longer lived with my grandfather. He was much older and had suffered a few more strokes. However, I visited him whenever I could.

I was able to buy a car and live in a tiny apartment near my parents. My schedule during the week was full because of my teaching and waitressing work. Weekends were devoted to church and the advertising gigs. I dated occasionally, but my focus was on finishing my master degree in education. Parties in the desert still were a part of my life, as I met many friends attending the university. One night stands out, in particular. A classmate encouraged me to accept a date with a fraternity buddy of his for one of these 'boondocker' fests. The party was loud, but the band was good and dancing under the stars was energizing. The drive back was not. My date had consumed a great deal of beer, and though I offered to drive back on the dangerous Gate's Pass mountain road, he reassured me he 'had it.' This was untrue. He was shakey at best. Each time I tried to grab the wheel so we didn't careen off the cliff, he would slap my hand away. I began to pray to God and my 'friends' to keep us safe. Miraculously, the next time our right wheel left the outside of the cliff we did not dip. It was as if we had hit a 'wall' of some kind and bounced back. I was astonished; my date was too out of it to notice. Each time the wheels left the road, we bounced back. This continued until we were safely down and off the cliff.

At the first gas station, I demanded to get out. I called a taxi and was soon home. I relived the mountain drive over and over as I tried to fall asleep. Either God or my Bright Friends had intervened. It hadn't been the first time, of this I was certain. Some people call them 'guardian angels'. Whatever or whoever, I had one on that night for sure. On several other occasions, I had felt an invisible hand on my back, even a metaphorical hand on my back, steering me in a certain life-direction.

Although I didn't remember many specifics of the

missing hours during the mountain visits, I did recall bits and pieces of 'lessons' transferred. Good was more powerful than evil, and that I should be careful what I wish for. In truth, I was so busy I couldn't dwell on the mysterious events in my life, such as the mountain visits. I clung to my family, my friends (the earth ones) and my faith. I did not actively think about my other 'friends', the Bright ones, during waking hours. I was on my destined path and it was speeding up. Through it all I knew that God and my Bright Friends were never far away. If I needed help, I called upon God through prayer and my Bright Friends through thoughts. They never failed to answer.

"My Eureka Moment Came Forty Years Later"

Once I was married I devoted my life to family, friends and a career in educational publishing. In fact, almost immediately upon leaving Arizona I put all visitation memories behind a metaphorical curtain in my mind. It seemed there was no place for them in my new life. Occasionally I would resurrect them, in particular if an article appeared in The New York Times about the improbability of intelligent life on other planets, solar systems and galaxies. It was easier not to say anything to the contrary. In the early 1970s high-powered telescopes had not yet calculated the number of observable galaxies in our universe. Today this number has been established as over 225 billion observable galaxies. The probability of there being intelligent life elsewhere is now a mathematical certainty. However, we are still being encouraged to deny this.

Forty years after leaving Arizona two major life events occurred: I got divorced and I became a grandmother. Both of these events were responsible for my beginning a journal once my memories came flooding back. Although my former spouse had been supportive of all my writing endeavors, I would never have started a book about my visitation experiences while still married. This was a solitary journey; not one

I could share while partnered. Also, when I became a grandmother for the first time in 2012, the bond of love that grew that first year was amazingly familiar. It mirrored the love I had felt during the early days of visitation with my Bright Friends. It was primal. In the spring of 2013, while returning on the Henry Hudson Parkway to the Bronx after an afternoon with my grandchild, I had a Eureka moment. I was in a taxi, quite saddened that I had to say goodbye to the baby for a while, when a 'curtain' lifted in my mind. I remembered the anguish on both our parts whenever a visitation ended and I had to leave my Bright Friends. Our love was primal; exactly the same as that I felt for my grandchild. It suddenly began to make sense; to fit together.

In addition, in December of 2012 I had visited my cousin on the west coast for the holiday. The night before my return, we were having dinner in the Cheesecake Factory. He asked me a question. "Would you ever considering writing about your 'friends'?" Suddenly I remembered how I had a premonition that during this journey, someone would ask me something weighty; something, if I said 'yes', would cost me a great deal personally. Now, I knew what that question was. I had an entire flight home to begin considering it.

"Messages of Love"

I always thought I didn't remember as much about the mountain visits compared to what I remembered about the Early Years 1-10 and the Harvesting Years 11-19. I know now that's untrue. I remember a great deal, much of it since my epiphany in 2013. A great deal of information was given me, or 'taught', during those three mysterious missing hours on countless Sundays between 1967 and 1972. Most of the lessons dwelt with love being more powerful than hate and good being more powerful than evil. Sometimes I listened to the messages while in the clear sarcophagus in the vast mountain chamber; other times I actually accompanied a human-type mentor while we travelled to troubled places on the planet. These were areas torn by centuries, even thousands of years, of unresolved hate and unrest. We looked 'down' upon the areas, ravaged by continual war and now wallowing in poverty and disease. Ironically, many of these areas were naturally rich in gems, minerals and metals such as gold and silver. However, the people never had a chance to organize themselves enough during peaceful periods to benefit from the areas' natural resources. Only a few warlords and their families and crews benefited. Many times illegal drugs and alcohol had been introduced to maintain the subjugation of these embattled peoples. Legacies of defeat their children had little chance of escaping. That's the way those in charge wanted it.

My mother noticed I had become very tolerant of people during my final years in Tucson, the five years I was compelled to go to the same mountain area on many Sunday afternoons and lose three hours of my time. I never questioned why I continued to drive to this specific location far out on Ajo Way or Ajo Road. It seemed absolutely logical for me to take a ride out there. Even when my mother questioned me about where I went and what I did, I simply told her 'I went for a ride in the desert'. Her curiousity about my mysterious drives was overshadowed by the marked changes in my attitudes towards my friends. Mother always was suspicious of the intentions of others if she thought they were trying to take advantage of me. She would constantly tell me that, "Not everyone is good, Karen." I would answer her by saying, "I know mom, but I prefer to see their good side rather than their bad side." She wasn't buying it, and we agreed to disagree on this point. She really thought I was blind to the way of the world. I wasn't. I always remembered a line from "The Diary of Anne Frank" right before her family was captured by the Nazis. She wrote, "I still believe that people are really good at heart." Even after listening to horrific accounts of the war on the radio and from the friends that were hiding them, Anne Frank never lost her belief in the goodness of human nature. She had kept her soul.

Compared to the scholars of the world, I am very low on the scale of those capable of transmitting lessons of good. I have acted in less than noble ways during brief portions of my life; ways I wish I could take back. I never broke the Ten Commandments, but I did become desensitized to the suffering of others during a period in my life when everything I needed was at my fingertips. Everything except redemption. For that, my life would have to change drastically. And it would.

the author
NYC
May 2013

Los Angeles, CA
the author
Dec. 2013

the
author
New York
City
1995-6

Part Four

'The Time Jumpers'

My Bright Friends, those special beings that visited me regularly the first twenty-five years of my life, were time jumpers. They had the technology that allowed them to travel beyond the boundaries of time and visit me from the future. When I first told my internist about the visits, he asked me where I thought they were from. I replied, "I think it's more relevant to ask 'when' they are from before 'where' they are from." It is possible that they are a future version of us now. Perhaps even both types are future versions of us: the ones that look human and the little, gray/blue ones.

Obviously the implications of this technology are exhilarating and frightening. If it is used for 'good/well-intentioned' purposes all is well. It also carries with it the potential to wreck havoc and cause trouble in the wrong hands. During these past five years of recollection, I often thought that many, if not all, paranormal experiences fit this criterion. Just as we today entertain ourselves with reality shows and shows about activities caught on security cameras, future humans may have the ultimate reality/entertainment shows due to time travel.

I do not say this lightly. My Bright Friends were wonderful and benevolent. I believe they were and are researchers, scientists and sociologists. The information they gather is used to better humankind and their world. Even the harvesting of my DNA, ova and breast tissue is for the betterment of lives in their world. However, during the final years, the mountain visits, information was transferred to me that though my friends were good, there were 'others' who were not well-intentioned. These others used future technology for personal gain, driven by greed. Just as criminals in our world today do the same.

I believe, also, that strict regulations, guidelines and licensing permits are attached to future time travel. As in our world, there are individuals who, for a price, will do what it takes to circumvent these restrictions and put the technology in the wrong hands. It is inevitable; the classic opening of Pandora's Vase (or Pandora's Box as it is more commonly referred to).

I am still remembering my countless visits and having epiphanies. It is a never-ending process. One that will stay with me for as long as I am alive or for as long as my mind remains clear in my elder years. I have the ability to recall my visits and not fear being burned at the stake as would have been the case three or four hundred years ago. However, I still fear those who today benefit from our ignorance about UFOs and those who remember being visited. We are still viewed suspiciously by many. It is true that many others today have open minds wanting more information from those of us who were visited. It is for these individuals that I continue to record my memories, recollections and epiphanies. May God bless us all and help us use our knowledge for the betterment of our world and other worlds yet to be discovered.

'Rearranging Molecules... Empathetically'

My Bright Friends, those wonderful beings who visited me frequently when I lived in Tucson, Arizona, I assumed were from the future. Perhaps they were us or variations of us in future years. One of their frequent communications to me was, 'We are related; we are family'. I could see the resemblance in the human looking ones. Even the little gray/blue ones felt amazingly like family to me. I loved them very much. I was privy to their advanced technology; sometimes, they would even 'explain' it to me. For example, when the ships would 'jump' from one point to another instead of travelling in a straight line, they showed me what I now know today is a GPS grid. Apparently they could jumble molecules around and send them from one location to another. We, they and me, were some of the molecules they jumped. I remember a shudder and a boom accompanying our jumping from location to location. My nose would often bleed as a result, and they would be very concerned. I would sit on the infirmary table with my head held back showing them how I could stop the bleeding. For some reason, my four year old efforts touched them immensely and they emanated their love for me.

Their advanced technology also allowed them to

'walk through walls' and set up protective 'shields' around the ship and even the individuals in the ground crews (usually made up of the little guys). I've written before about the reactions of my physicians upon my telling them of these visitations. Many wanted to know 'where' they were from. I believe most of my visitors were us from a future time. Perhaps some of them were even genetically related to me. In theory, they could have been both my ancestors and my descendants. Fair hair and gray/green and gray/blue eyes dominate my genetic ancestry. Many of my visitors had this coloring, and I even thought their features looked much like mine.

I was not supposed to remember my visits, but I did. Early on, my Bright Friends realized this. That was when they sent the messenger to my room to 'explain' to me how they might not be able to visit me anymore because I was remembering. I was shattered and began to cry hysterically. I loved them very much and the thought of them not being in my life was unbearable, even though I was four or five years old. It was communicated to me that on the condition that I not tell anyone, they would continue to visit me. I readily agreed. They explained that no one would believe me and I would be told I had been dreaming. However, they were emphatic that I was not dreaming and that our visits were real. I communicated back that I knew that already: I could smell the desert when they took me into the desert to board the ships.

For some reason, our society continues to repress acknowledging their existence and presence in our lives. I don't know exactly why, but I believe it has something to do with economics and thus power. Many times discussions about aliens and UFOs center around an apocalyptic alien agenda. Based on my experiences this is a false threat. My Bright Friends were benevolent, wise and loving. However, they did indicate there were others who were not as well-intentioned. Never did I feel a threat of any kind from these wonderful relatives of ours. I only hope I live to see the day we can look to them with hope and love. I am almost seventy now; perhaps I may never see this. I do know in the not too distant future, we will have to accept this very real part of our world because our own advancements in technology will prove beyond a doubt of their existence and presence in our lives since our beginnings here on earth.

It is now 2016 A.D. I have dedicated the past four years to writing a memoir about being visited by those I called my Bright Friends from 1947 to 1972, when I lived in Tucson, Arizona the first twenty-five years of my life. Perhaps the one most common occurrence during those many visits was the presence of a brilliant white light surrounding my friends when they visited me outside the protective environment of their spaceships; such as in my bedroom, or when we stood outside the ships preparing to board. I have come to many conclusions and epiphanies during these years of recollection. One is that I know my friends were being truthful when they communicated to me that 'we were related; we were family.' Another epiphany was when I realized that they, my visiting friends, very likely came from the future. They could manipulate the boundaries of space and time through their advanced technology. Someday, I know, we will be able to do the same. When time travel will be a possibility for us, then the debate about whether or not UFOs and 'aliens' visited our planet in prior years will be put to rest. The answer will be 'yes', and the unlikely conclusion is that a future form of us were the ones who did the visiting. Those years are yet to come. For now, we are surrounded by speculation... and for me, the bright light.

Although I am not a physicist or scientist of any kind, I am sure that the brilliant light which surrounded my Bright Friends protected them in some way. My best guess can be explained using a deep sea diving analogy. Just as divers who sink to dangerous ocean depths in the quest for exploration and then must decompress on their way back to their natural sea level to avoid the bends, time travelers need the bright light to help them 'decompress' to the changes in gravity, barometric pressure and air quality which would occur during an unnatural change in space/time conditions. Even when I was taken aboard the crafts, I would go through what I felt was a cool 'misting' tunnel. After I had traversed the tunnel, I would emerge in their crafts, comfortably breathing their air and moving about their 'time/space' environment. At times, my nose would bleed and my visitors would be worried for me.

It is and has been exhausting trying to write down my memories and experiences. I do so because it helps vindicate the lifetime of silence I felt I had to live due to the naysayers of my day. We are approaching the time, in the not distant future, when as I wrote above, our own technology will answer the debate surrounding the existence of UFOs and far away visitors contacting us. I have always known the answer. My silence has been isolating and lonely at times, however the thought of my life without the presence of my Bright Friends would be less loving, rich and exhilarating.

'Chimps to Humans to Beyond Humans'

Last night I was reading a fictional novel whose plot involved transgenic experiments and the problems they create. It was written by a well-known doctor, and I found it fascinating. A premise for the experiments was that when humans split from apes or chimpanzees six million years ago, we (the humans) developed the ability for speech. Apes and chimpanzees do not have the organs necessary for speech. In the novel the implication was that they also did not have the capacity for language, even non-verbal language. I disagree with this, since they seem to communicate brilliantly with one another. Regardless of whether they had the capacity for language, the truth was and is that chimps do not speak as we do. Their thought processes function on some kind of communal level, as they usually exist in a community.

My Bright Friends did not speak to me...ever...during twenty-five years of visitations. Our communication was beyond words. It was comprehensive, primal and layered. To reduce it to mental telepathy seems limiting as there were emotional components as well. I could 'feel' what they were feeling. As I've written in previous pages, it was always communicated to me that I was related to them, or we were...humans. 'We were family' was how it was transferred. They used many analogies for me. For instance, the first time I was taken to board a ship, they used the analogy of 'it's like one of your airplanes.' Ironically, in my toddler state I had never seen an airplane, much less taken a ride in one. They had no way of knowing this, or perhaps their instructions were to use this analogy with me. I still was able to understand this comparison as the message was very comprehensive and detailed. For whatever reason, during my visits with my Bright Friends I was able to engage in this type of non-verbal, highly effective communication. Apparently the ability to go beyond words exists in us now. We just do not know how to awaken it, fortunately for existing communications giants. Their empires would suffer greatly when we will unlock it, as it is a matter of time before we do.

Although I will be long dead when the next split for humans occurs, it will happen. Perhaps the smaller, child-like beings I met are the result of this next genetic split. Just like in our present time, both chimpanzees and humans exist in their own societies. This explains why I saw both kinds: humans and the 'evolved humans'. Sadly, it seems the jungles the chimps live in are being ravaged for economic gain resulting in the endangerment of their species. Is this the reason why these future humans are coming back and visiting us now? Do they want us to protect our world so that future generations will be able to enjoy it as we do? My Bright Friends felt I was 'fortunate'; perhaps I live in a world they cannot live in.

Time travel technology will be present in the world of these future beings. Obviously, this poses a threat to our present society and the humans who enjoy the billions they have made by cornering the energy and communications markets. For us regular folk, time travel is exhilarating; for the money barons it is terrifying and threatening. It would shatter their power base and even the playing field. I fully believe this is why the money behind the military blocking of any official acknowledgement of the existence of UFOS and visitations by advanced beings is so strong. The threat is not that the visitors want to harm us, but that the knowledge they can transfer to us will destroy the status quo.

The truth will come out. Our visitors, my Bright Friends, want it to come out peacefully, which is why they don't push it forward, which they could do. We have to be ready to accept it. We are not ready yet.

'Beneath the Earth and Above the Heavens'

At the time of the next split (or jump) in the evolution of our human lineage, what will be the state of the earth? Those of us on earth now in 2016 A.D. are witness to the natural habitats of many species being destroyed because of pollution, desalinization of our oceans or deforestation of our forests. Will we, humans, be the next species to lose our habitat, the planet earth? Of course, it's possible we will have a back-up plan and establish alternative 'habitats' possibly fathoms below sea level in our oceans, or deep in the caverns of mountain ranges on the surface of the earth or far out in 'space station communities' sharing real estate with the constellations.

During the final five years of my visitations in Tucson, Arizona (1967-1972), I would drive myself to the foothills of the Santa Rita mountain range to the southeast of Tucson. Once there I would park my car and check the time. The next thing I remembered would be three hours later. Flashbacks of being deep inside the mountains during those missing hours in a vast cavern are still with me. I believe for the smaller future versions of humans, refuge in our mountain caverns provides an environment that they can live in due to their fragile bodies with no hair and very little pigmentation for protection against solar rays.

Farming food products will continue in a limited fashion on the surface of the earth and in a new way deep beneath our oceans. How we continue to feed our species, whether they are in space or on earth or beneath it will challenge our descendants. Medical advancements will continue, with ever increasing laws and restrictions regarding the taking of any bodily DNA including blood for testing. Blood testing will be accomplished by a small amount of skin cells transferred to litmus paper. Any illegal procuring of human DNA or blood will be dealt with harshly, with draconian punishments. For this reason, I believe black markets will flourish in pirate ships returning to earth in our time to harvest human DNA and blood. My Bright Friends communicated to me that although they were good, there were others in their time and world who were not. The way it was communicated was that they were not as 'well-intentioned'. My Bright Friends also would emphasize that good was always more powerful than evil.

Crop circles and animal mutilations baffle us today. Again, I think these activities are carried on by those engaged in the illegal poaching of the resources available on 'our earth' which will not be available on a future 'earth' or in a future world. In addition, many times groups of eye witnesses have seen a flurry of lights in night skies, seemingly involved in a game of chase. Are these future cops chasing down illegal

DNA poachers and dealers? Although information was transferred to me, I do not live in their world. My deductions and conclusions are drawn from my experiences with them and from the information about their world which was transferred to me.

The question of religion and the 'God particle' always is a part of my work in preparing this memoir. I believe that the practice of religion will continue in the future. I am not a theologian therefore I do not want to dwell on this, as I am not qualified. As for me, my experiences have never shaken my religious beliefs. In fact, I feel closer to God as a result. I want to live out my final years in humility and service to God. If my recollections will help future humans, then I will do my best to continue working on this memoir until my dying day.

'On the Ships"

I try to revisit my most vivid memories periodically during the transcribing of this memoir for various reasons. One reason is that those memories are the trigger points for me remembering more about my twenty-five years of visits. One extremely vivid and exciting memory recalls a visit when my Bright Friends took me to the bridge to watch as we journeyed through the night skies. This wasn't an isolated incident, as when they finished testing me in the little classroom or taking some biological DNA samples I was allowed to follow them as they performed other functions. This one time I was taken to the bridge and allowed to sit on a platform so that I could see out the windows or portals. Suddenly the night sky lit up with endless strong light. This was accompanied by a slight shudder of the ship and a boom. Looking out the portal I saw that night had turned to day. The next day I tried to tell my mother that I knew how 'dawn came'. I was only three or four and my account of being taken aboard a flying craft that resembled our airplanes by a group of Bright Friends shook my mother to her core. It wasn't that she didn't believe me; in fact I think she did. She was flooded with motherly concern when she realized that she could do nothing to protect me from the beings who took me on this journey, but she could do something about the people we lived with.

"Karen, you must not tell anyone about this. Do you understand?" She was gripping my shoulders and looking intently at me with her panic-stricken eyes.

"Okay mommy. Don't worry, my friends are nice to me."

"It's not your friends I'm worried about. Just don't tell anyone. Promise me." She was distraught.

Mother was not the only one concerned about how my social group would react to my being visited. Once my Bright Friends realized it, they sent a messenger to convince me that the only way to ensure they visit me again would be for me to promise I wouldn't tell anyone. As they communicated it...

"It would be better if you didn't tell anyone about your visits. They will tell you that what you are remembering is a dream. We want you to know that these are not dreams. These visits are really happening." I communicated back to the messenger that I already knew that because...

"I could smell the desert on the way to board the ships."

Sometimes my nose would bleed badly during a voyage. I remember sitting on the infirmary table with a 'human' being on one side of me and one of the little guys (the uber-human beings) on the other.

They would smile at me as I turned my head back and pinched my nostrils in an attempt to stem the blood flow.

On some ships there were labs with botanical samples of desert plant life and geological rock collections. I loved being in these labs and shown the different cuttings and semi-precious gems. But what I really loved were the small, blue classrooms with the smooth tables and chairs. I would sit with the little guys, who I thought (at the time) were other children. We would play games…I thought. I always remember it looked like 'rain' outside. Perhaps we were using clouds for cover during the visits.

At the end of these early ship visits, I would beg my Bright Friends to let me live with them. It wasn't that my parents weren't good to me. With these friends I was treated like precious cargo. I was 'important' to them in a really special way. As young as I was, I realized this. I would cry at the end of each visit, and I could feel the sadness of my friends, as well. Now, seven decades later, I still love them.

'Now Comes the DNA Proof'

His name is Cyril H. Wecht. He is a pathologist. His career has spanned over fifty years and 14,000 cases. His testimony has been used by prosecutors and defending attorneys in courts of law. He was called upon to investigate the assassination of President John F. Kennedy. That was not his most famous case. More recently, he participated in examining the DNA of an alien being. His findings stated that the DNA was 'humanoid'.

Those who continue to dispute the fact that UFOs and aliens are a part of our world, the entire world, are becoming desperate. A back-up plan (if they cannot convince the population that UFOs and aliens are a hoax) is to portray these strange lifeforms as hostile invaders. Finding that they are related to us does not help their campaigns. Add to this, the advancements in quantum physics and the soon to be reality of travel through worm holes to new dimensions of time and space...well, you can see the conundrum.

Of course, even with 'proof' emerging rapidly not only to the reality of these beings but also to the technology which allows them to visit us from the future the only recourse is to advance their claims that they must be hostile and wish us no good. Only those of us who have been visited by benevolent future relatives of ours can provide eye-witness accounts disproving these primitive generalizations. I cannot say that 'some' of those visiting us are not ill-intentioned, as I was given knowledge that some 'other', non-benevolent beings do come and illegally poach our DNA. However, I also was given the very strong communication that the 'good ones' always are more 'powerful' than the 'ill-intentioned' ones. It saddened my visitors when they had to communicate this to me. I was an adult at the time, about 20-23 years old. It was during one of my 'mountain visits'.

Today, in a court of law, eye witness accounts are taken seriously. Next to DNA they are the most powerful tool in the arsenal of prosecutors and defense attorneys. When it comes to those of us who have seen and communicated with these beings, for over two decades in my case, a double standard exists. I am a former teacher, with no criminal record. I believe in God and attend church services. I've raised a family and am a grandmother. I do not drink or take hallucinogenic drugs. Yet, my testimony today wouldn't be listened to seriously, I believe. I may not be mocked as I would have been in the 1950s, or burned at the stake as I would have been in the 17th century. Still, it is exhausting and troubling being treated as if I am making up my experiences.

Why was I visited? Location, location, location. My birth in 1947 in Tucson, Arizona was key, but it was not the only factor. I believe these future humans have a genetic map of our planet, for many time periods... not just now. I had some type of genetic history that they needed. During the 'harvesting years: 11 – 19 years of age', my ova, breast tissue and other DNA was constantly taken. As a result, my right breast had to be surgically reconstructed when I was 20. My doctors said it looked like I had had a mastectomy. I am almost 70 years of age now, and I was able to nurse my children. I have no ill feelings about the harvesting of my DNA. As they communicated to me 'we are related: we are family'.

I realize the fear of those in power, who risk losing a financial base when new technology in communications and time travel emerge. Change is inevitable. In future years, factories with artificial wombs for every species will be a major industry. It is only logical that our DNA is essential to them.

‘Sailing On Seas; Flying In Space; Jumping Through Time’

Humans have tried, successfully, throughout their evolution to manipulate their surroundings. Early Bronze Age men constructed primitive boats; this was the beginning of trade and exploration as we can see in subsequent ancient Mesopotamia, Egypt and Greece. Thousands of years later, humans invented airplanes to navigate the skies. Not that many years need to pass from our present development for us to control time/space dimensions and boundaries. We will ‘jump’ through these passages someday as effortlessly as we sail the oceans or the skies; it is just around the corner for us.

When humans conquered the seas, and constructed more powerful sailing vessels, they were able to travel to exotic lands. These early sailors saw amazing wonders and cultural differences. The exotic trade cargo they brought back was sometimes procured without the permission of the indigenous populations. In the 17th century, Captain Cook did not ask permission from the inhabitants of the south sea islands he sailed to and plundered. With their superior technology, Cook and his crew could protect themselves from hostile island inhabitants defending their families and their environment. In his own world Captain Cook was a good family man with six children. He was not a criminal nor a cruel person. Yet to the people of the islands he 'discovered', he was terrifying; possessing technology that rendered them helpless and full of amazement. Among his crew were scientists and botanists. Exotic animals, plants and produce, which would be invaluable back in England, were put into the cargo hold...without the permission of the original island inhabitants, or the permission of the animals for that matter.

The parallels between what Captain Cook and his crew did in the quest for discovery and progress, which was not a crime at the time, and how today's abductees feel about the biological harvesting of their DNA, ova and sperm by alien visitors is clear. They feel violated by the aliens doing what may simply be a licensed or legal expedition in their world. We can look to another more recent scientific expedition for more parallels: pharmacological journeys to the rain forests of South America. Deep in these lush jungles, hidden in indigenous plant and insect life are DNA components for tomorrow's miracle drugs. However, the risk to native populations, as well as the journeying scientists, is high. One participant with a cold can wipe out entire tribes. Spanish Conquistadors unwittingly transmitted disease to indigenous South American peoples in their quest for cities of gold. The cooperation and assistance of the indigenous populations in Amazon rain forests is essential to the success of the expeditions. They know how to scale the tall trees for necessary plants or cut a path through dense forestation with machetes. Usually, the cooperative relationship between the explorers and the native people works out well for both of them. This is the case when these operations are conducted ethically and with strict regulations. However, we all know that pirates and unlicensed poachers work secretively, as the products they gather bring huge profits in black markets. The South American cocaine drug cartel is the most egregious example of our time.

It is inevitable that future pirates and poachers will be using time travel technology to journey back to earth, during our time, and illegally harvest human DNA, ova and sperm. I believe this is the reason why my experiences with 'benevolent visitors' are markedly different from many other abductees' experiences. I'm positive that Betty and Barney Hill, the couple that were abducted in the 1960s, were the victims of just such unlicensed poachers. It seems, no matter how evolved we are, criminals flourish.

'Will Time Travel Cancel the Finality of Death?'

A great deal of information was transferred to me during my 'mountain visit' period. I was a teacher at the time, and my car was a blue VW hatchback. About twice a month, on Sundays after church and lunch with my parents, I would take drives in the desert and foothills southwest of Tucson. As I have written many times before, I parked my car and checked the dashboard clock. The next time I looked at the clock, three hours had passed. In the days following these visits, pieces of memories would drift back to me. I was inside a clear sarcophagus (the only word that describes it) deep in the mountain, and I was not alone. I was one among hundreds in a vast cavern. During my time in this sarcophagus I was 'fed' information. My essays reflect the information I was given concerning who my visitors were, the kind of world they lived in and the reasons for their visitations to us. I now believe I was not supposed to access much of this information until later in my life (now), when I had a better overview of the world I lived in.

During the 'mountain visit' years spanning 1967-1972, I was 20 -25 years old. These would be the last years I lived in Tucson, as the following year I would relocate to New York City and get married.

Included in my flashbacks, were some very unusual 'memories'. I had the very odd notion at the time that how fun it would be to travel back to ancient civilizations and observe how they lived. I had never been an avid history buff. Thanks to a voracious reading appetite and several humanities classes, I had a general knowledge and mild interest in some ancient cultures. Certainly ancient Greece was of interest as I was of Greek heritage on both parent's sides. However, Hellenistic Greece was not the period I envisioned. It was ancient Egypt or Mesopotamia that I could 'see' myself in. I was always a voyeur, never a participant in their lives. My thoughts at the time concluded that these were simply 'what if' daydreams. Now, many decades later and after the retrieval of countless buried memories, I wonder if those were really just 'daydreams'. Perhaps my visitors took me on some 'special' journeys before our visits ended.

As I've written in prior essays, time travel will someday be as accessible to future voyagers as airplane travel is today. Strict regulations will surround the use of this technology and hopefully prevent the misuse of it. Still, I cannot help but wonder if someday we will be able to visit those beloved family members and dear friends who have died (assuming, of course, that medical science has not conquered the finality of death). Might we even be able to 'bring' them to a future world? The implications are disturbing at best. Grandparents coming back to grandchildren who might exceed them in age? Or citizens from prior generations experiencing 'culture shock' at a future world that bears little resemblance to the one they left and is disturbing in its arrogance.

As we advance in technology and break down barriers, we also open a Pandora's Box of unimaginable ethical problems. Today we can create and sustain human embryos in vitro. Advances in medicine allow us to replace body parts, including organs, and rejuvenate cells by genetic modification. It is inevitable that we are marching towards a full sustaining of life functions in humans. I am not a doctor but the writing is on the wall. Where are all these people going to live? Moreover, will they be happy? A life cycle is part of nature. What happens when a life cycle is altered and extended and not allowed to complete its natural end? Perhaps in appearance a person might look normal, but what could be going on in their psyche? Whole new areas of psychological therapies will have to be developed to help these future Frankenstiens. It will be a New World indeed.

'...Cancelling the Finality of Death'

If I am correct about the eventual reality of time travel, what are some possible uses for this powerful technology?

1. In criminal investigations, will the officers and investigators be able to backtrack to just before a crime occurred and follow the victim until they meet up with the perpetrator?
2. In terminal cancer cases, will physicians be able to track a patient and watch the progression of a disease; ultimately pinpointing any triggers or contributing collateral pre-existing conditions in the cells or the patient?
3. For those individuals who cannot 'live forever' for some reason, will family members have the ability to 'visit' with them, and be able to share any family news the diseased may have missed?

The above are possible 'good' uses for time travel. What would the misuse of this technology do?

1. Will individuals from the future be able to simulate 'ghosts' and frighten people living in our present time for entertainment purposes?

2. Would relatives of incarcerated criminals be able to go back in time and help them escape?
3. Could we change history? What if the residents of Pompeii in 79 A.D. were shown proof of the impending eruption of Vesuvius?

I cannot responsibly predict the uses of time travel technology. I do know that extremely strict rules for the uses of the technology exist. The reason I know this is that when my Bright Friends began visiting me in my early childhood years, they didn't expect me to remember. When they realized I was remembering they communicated to me, "We don't know why you are remembering. People usually don't remember." Apparently, one rule or law concerning time travel is that those being visited will not be aware of the visits. As in my case, things do not always follow the expected plan or path. The original purposes for a time travel visit might be sanctioned by future rulers, however the unexpected variables are the most exciting and dangerous results. Perhaps my unexpected memory of those early visits ensured two more decades with my Bright Friends coming to see me.

I am not a physicist, however from what I have read about worm holes and areas around the earth that might be more easily accessed by inter-dimension travelers the possibility is that time travel will come with its own, built-in restrictions here on earth. Of course, as the technology of time travel progresses I believe we will be able to expand the natural vortexes on the planet to cover greater areas. Ultimately, we will be able to replicate the geological and atmospheric conditions necessary to house a natural vortex, making time travel available regardless of locations. I base my theory on what happened with DNA testing for forensic use. In the infancy stages of DNA testing, a substantial amount of undamaged DNA was needed. After one or two decades, scientists were able to artificially expand and repair even a miniscule amount of DNA, making it viable to be tested. In theory, this should be the case with the new technology of time travel, taking it beyond its earthly boundaries to anywhere on or off the planet. I won't be taking advantage of any future time travel, but I've had very good friends who have.

‘Sharing Yields Questions’

Questions immediately were asked by those I began sharing my experiences with. Here are some of those questions and their answers.

1. Why were the second group of visitors not as loving as the first?
   Using the analogy of kindergarten teachers compared to high school teachers best illustrates how I perceived my visitors in both these groups. In kindergarten my teachers were loving and nurturing. In high school my teachers were ‘instructing’ me rather than ‘nurturing’ me. During the second part of my visitations, the harvesting years 11 – 19, I always was with a group. I felt I was naked or unclothed and freezing, as I walked through corridors with this group. I also thought perhaps I was in school and I forgot to get dressed before leaving the house. However, as impersonal as this group of visitors was, upon my return home after a harvesting procedure a ‘loving’ being accompanied me and stayed with me as I regained feeling in my body shortly before falling asleep. I could feel their love and sometimes thought a current boyfriend

of mine was watching me sleep…'again'. This pattern occurred over and over again during my adolescence: the pattern of being taken, having procedures and then returning home to be watched by a caring being as I slept. The ones doing the harvesting were simply scientists.

2. Why didn't my mother stay up at night and keep watch over me when I was an infant after finding me out of my crib and sleeping on the floor many mornings? She did, however either she had no memory of how I ended up on the floor many mornings, or I was safe in my crib other mornings. She had no defenses against their superior technology. It would be similar to monkeys living in a preserve. If the researchers need to immunize some of the infants, they must take them away from their mothers temporarily. The only way they can do this is to tranquilize the mothers. It is a procedure we use often with animals living in preserves, and it is done in the best interest of mother monkeys, the infant monkeys and the group which provides and protects their living environment. I hope this is clear, as I am not a researcher or scientist.
3. One friend of mine was very interested in the procedure used when the visitors took

samples of breast tissue from me. I was not conscious during entire procedures. If I 'awoke' during a harvesting endeavor I was put back down immediately, as a patient in one of our operating rooms would be if they awoke during an operation. My memories are not always sequential, and my visitors tried their best to have me forget the experiences entirely.

In addition to the above questions, I've been asked if 'time was different when I was on the ships', 'if I had any ideas where they came from' and 'what they looked like in detail'. Time seemed to be suspended during my visits and in my adult years (the mountain visits) I would be surprised that several hours were missing every time I was 'called' to the mountain locations. As for 'where they might be from', as I told the doctor who asked this, 'it's more relevant to ask when they are from, rather than where.' Obviously, if I ever publish my memoir I will be flooded with questions. I will be able to answer some; many I will not be able to answer. I have had to live every day not knowing the answers to a lifetime of questions. I know how frustrating it is.

'DNA Factories: Genetics As Currency'

During the Harvesting Years (11-19 years of age), I was usually in a sleep/like state. I remember walking the circular corridors of the ships along with many other adolescents. I was wearing very little and it was extremely cold. At times it felt as if I was walking the halls of my high school with my friends. Where were my books? Why wasn't I dressed for school? Then, I would realize I wasn't in school, but it didn't matter. I was somewhere I was supposed to be. One by one we would enter different 'classrooms' (actually exam rooms). Everything seemed stark and functional; there was no decoration. However, one 'chart' (more like a photo slide of a chart) was in all the rooms. It looked like a map of the desert I lived in. It was a map: a genetic map. I thought it odd that a binary code was superimposed upon this map. I now know the markings I saw were not a binary code; they were DNA markers for genetic harvesting purposes. I was an adolescent in the 1960s, and I had no knowledge of DNA whatsoever. I did have knowledge of a binary number system, as I had been in a special math class in middle school. So, I thought a binary code was important to my Bright Friends for some reason. In my semi-conscious state, I didn't dwell too long on these curious charts.

Once I began writing about my visitations during the first twenty-five years of my life (1947-1972), my memories began to fall into place like jig saw puzzle pieces. This didn't happen overnight. There were many epiphanies along the way, when I would suddenly remember the totality of a visitation experience rather than just a snippet of memory about it. This process was deliberate and exhausting. I have tried to find analogies in our present time (the 21st century) to illustrate what happened to me in a way that would make sense to my readers. From time to time during the past five years, I have shared some of these pages and some of my drawings with friends. Their prescient questions have helped me understand how foreign and frightening some of my experiences seemed to them. In particular, the difference between the nurturing care my Bright Friends lavished on me during the Early Years (birth -10 years) and the clinical efficiency of the harvesting carried on by the second group of Bright Friends seemed incongruous. Some of my friends and readers felt the second group was 'uncaring'. I had to explain in better detail that what seemed uncaring to them was simply the way the second group handled routine procedures during a work shift. I don't have all the answers. In fact, my recollections cannot help but be subjective. I have almost no one to compare my experiences with. Once in a while someone might tell me that they 'saw' a UFO, yes even here in NYC. Other than that, I have met no one who remembers twenty-five years of sustained visitations by friendly beings. No one.

Some days writing about my experiences wears me to the bone. I have to save my energy in order to put the necessary effort into the completion of this memoir. I have to keep working on it until I feel it is as complete as it should be. And although I won't be alive to see it, some day inter-planetary stock markets will be trading DNA commodities as routinely as they do 'gold and silver' shares today. Of this, I am absolutely positive.

'Future Drugstore Geneticists'

In a previous essay, I put forth the idea that in the future DNA shares will be sold via inter-planetary stock markets. DNA enhancing products will be available as well at local pharmacies, as easily obtainable as vitamins are today. Future citizens will be able to ensure that before an embryo develops fully it has been genetically enhanced. Of course, this is a theory, and I am not a geneticist. However, since my DNA was of importance to my Bright Friends, and since they transferred information to me about what occurred and why, I feel I must write about it no matter how clumsy my efforts. How sacred human life will be in the future, I'm not sure. Today abortions are legal in many states. Executions are also legal in some states for capitol offenders. It is a difficult, sticky wick that will not be any easier to decide upon no matter how evolved we become. Therefore, how sacred will the building blocks of life (human genes) be in the future? I have no doubt that they will be a precious commodity whether sold through legal markets or black markets.

In the 5th century B.C., Hippocrates put forth the theory that the 'bricks and mortar' of human characteristics (our genes) were first transferred through the male donor, but after that the environment was responsible for the final genetic make-up of an individual (those genes that adapted and survived). Decades later, Aristotle refined Hippocrates 'bricks and mortar' theory of genetics, as did the many scholars that followed throughout the centuries including Mendel and Darwin. I wonder what they would think about the power 'drugstore geneticists' of the future would have.

I have thought long and hard about what genetic traits I carry that were desirable to my Bright Friends. I am sure it is not the color of my skin, eyes or hair. I believe that something in the genetics of my immune system is the draw. In fact, I'm positive about this. For me, it's a moot point. I was visited for a reason, and it wasn't only because I was born in the southwestern Arizona desert in 1947. Maybe I will figure it out before I die. Probably I won't. I can live with that... actually, I have to don't I?

'Two Past Midnight'

It is past midnight, two or three in the morning, when all is quiet and life replenishes with sleep. This is when I would be visited by those I never knew by name. They were and are my friends. They came in a flood of bright light and would take me from my childhood bed to gleaming ships in the desert. In the arms of one of the human types I would be carried on board. 'He' would place a hand over my eyes to shield them from the brilliant light. I peeked anyway. A message popped in my mind, 'It is like your airplanes.' Although I had never seen or been on an airplane, I understood what he meant. We went into the softly winding corridors, perfectly lit by filtered blue-yellow light. I sat at the little table in the classroom. Someone came and sat next to me; he was one of the 'other' types. He looked a little different than we, than humans, did. He was shorter, and he had no hair. I thought that was funny. He was sweet and kind and 'felt' human to me. I had a child's heart and still judged individuals with the innocence of that heart. He was kind, wise and he smiled a lot. My friends never 'spoke' to me with words, they would send me ideas in my mind. When I was with them I could communicate in this manner, as well. Their was an oval window in the little classroom.

Water appeared outside the window. I thought that everytime I was in this room, it rained outside. My time with them was indescribable. I felt a primal connection. I wouldn't feel this same connection until I became a grandmother sixty years later.

It is past midnight, two or three in the morning. I am sixteen years old. Someone is watching me sleep. Maybe they can help me. I can't move or say anything; I am paralyzed. 'It's alright; calm down. You will regain feeling soon.' This thought came in my mind. It came from the one who was watching me sleep. Who was he? He had great affection for me; he has known me since my birth. He won't let anything happen to me. I begin to feel my feet, my legs and finally I can move my mouth to speak. Then, I fall asleep and my body regenerates. He stays by me; I can feel his love. I am safe.

It is past midnight, two or three in the morning. I am sixty-nine years old. I say my prayers to God, thanking the almighty for my every blessing and praying that all the children on earth and their families and everyone is safe, free from hunger and want and watched over. It is a childlike wish, and now that I am older I know that everyone is not safe, or free from hunger and want. It was the wish of those who visited me the first twenty-five years of my life. They never really left me, as I knew they were with me somehow as I first became a wife, then a mother and then a grandmother. My life's road was not always easy, but I never suffered from hunger or abject poverty. I had different hills to climb. My friends, I called them my Bright Friends, had transferred messages to me throughout those years of visitations. They hoped that we, humans, would work to help others out of the chains of poverty and despair. This was a very important wish of theirs. A young messenger, a human looking being, visited me in my childhood. They allowed me to be fully awake for this visit. He transferred this thought to me before leaving, 'you are fortunate.' Indeed, I have been. I know he meant that I was not born into poverty and despair. I had a chance...and for those of us with this chance, it was important we try and make the world a better, safer place for all.

It is past midnight. I don't have much time left. I hope I make a difference.

'Difficult Journeys Home: Falling Through Energy Tunnels'

During the Harvesting Years (11-19 years of age), I was on my own when traveling to and from the visits. I don't remember being taken up to the ships, however I remember vividly returning to my bedroom at the end of the visits. As I've written many times, my Bright Friends did their best so that I would not remember the visits. They were puzzled as to why I had such clear recollections. In fear of erasing my daytime (earthtime) memories, they could do very little more to block my memory. When I would awaken during a procedure, I would immediately be put out again. The trips back home when all was finished were the most frightening for me.

It seemed I was standing at the edge of a cliff with nothing but endless black space beneath me. Suddenly I felt I was 'pushed' off the cliff. I then 'whooshed' through the darkness in a tunnel of light. The next thing I was conscious of was being in my own bed, paralyzed. Someone was watching me; someone who cared for me and was concerned about my well-being.

Although I had not been aware of it, I had to have passed through the walls of my house to reach my bed. Their technology was advanced enough to manipulate the molecular structure of solid walls. It is difficult for me, in my present time, to fully understand the scope of their command over their environment. I feel like a Bronze Age woman watching automatic doors open and close, not realizing what is actually happening. To me, it would appear as if a solid wall suddenly 'melted' to make an opening.

The way we, humans, interpret what we see during these visits is filtered through our background of experiences. Many abductees describe enormous, uncanny and frightening black eyes on the smaller, hybrid-human beings. Just as we wear masks and goggles when deep sea diving, these beings protect their eyes and face in the same way. Many abductees describe the goggles as a part of their anatomy. It's exactly like what primitive cave dwellers painted on the cave walls tens of thousands of years ago. They thought the space suits they drew actually were a part of the beings wearing them. In the Bible, Ezekial describes a 'flying chariot' with faces on the outside panels. Could he have been describing beings inside the spaceships looking out of portholes?

I have done my best to describe my experiences using analogies my readers can relate to. It is a very difficult process. I cannot separate my fear of falling from what still seems a mega-cliff when logically I know I was in an energy tunnel of sorts. I don't even know if my molecular structure was in one piece during the transfer. That thought always disturbs me. My friends did their best to put me out fully. It just wasn't enough in my case. However, they were always reassuring me...even as I fell.

'The Ka and the Ba of Our Souls'

During my final five years of residing in Arizona (1967-1972), I repeatedly drove to an isolated desert area in the foothills of the Santa Rita mountain range to the southwest of Tucson. Once there I would park my car and lose three hours of my life; I had no immediate memory of those visits. Only decades later the information that was transferred to me during those lost hours would begin to surface. This essay is the result of those delayed memories surfacing many decades later.

Advancements in genetic research are developing so rapidly we lose sight of how monumental and life-altering they truly are. Geneticists are now nurturing embryos developed from more than two parents. Stem cells are helping to correct genetic disabilities at primal levels, and it is now possible for parents to be able to choose the sex of future offspring as easily as choosing eye and hair color. What is next?

What if geneticists can identify and isolate the genetic DNA of the soul? The ancient Egyptians believed that the moment a person died the soul (the ka) separated from the body (the ba). Only prayers and incantations from The Book of the Dead could direct these two entities in their journey through the afterlife. After seventy years of life, I now believe our souls have as much chance of being isolated and identified through DNA and genetic research as any other genetic characteristic. The combination of genetic components and energy that will identify our 'souls' will differ only slightly from that of other human traits. I believe it will have more 'energy enabling' genomes than say eye or hair color. I am not a scientist, and I have no idea why I feel so strongly about how future genetic research will make it possible for scientists to identify a soul, but I know it will be possible. We have the basic knowledge now. Just as we have the basic knowledge for the development of time travel, so do we have the basic knowledge for the development of genetically identifying and isolating the DNA of our souls.

As recently as two hundred years ago, it would have seemed ludicrous for anyone to believe that a flying ship would be able to take people to not only a location on the other side of the world, but to that same location only the passengers would arrive there one day ahead of 'when' they left. We do not think of this as time travel, yet it proves that time travel is possible and that we are using the very first crude forms of it. It is the same with the genetic research that is being done today. Scientists collectively hold their breath and do not articulate the Pandora's Box that today's genetic research is opening. Misuse of this research will occur; of that I am certain. Consider the misuse of chemical warfare as recently as the Vietnam War. On a more individual level, many spouses have used over the counter poisons that were developed to kill vermin, to do away with their partners. The misuse of advanced weaponry is apparent in acts of terrorism whether at home or abroad. It is a sad footnote of our human condition that we use these advancements for personal vendettas rather than for the collective good.

I will not be around to see what will happen once the human 'soul' has been genetically identified. As with any powerful technology, the restrictions for the use of this knowledge will be strict. Hopefully, the general public will not have access to it. I hope that will be the case for time travel, as well. The implications for the misuse of that are bone-chilling. Time travel might be beneficial in some instances such as the identification of criminals and the prevention of murders; however, the flip side is also possible. God save us from ourselves.

‘Differing Accounts From Other Abductees and the Possible Explanations’

I have spent the past five years remembering and analyzing visits by ‘aliens’ during the first twenty-five years of my life. Today people are more willing to discuss their visitation experiences, and I compared aspects of my visits with differing accounts to the visits of others. The differences were dramatic.

In an account from Betty Hill (who along with her husband Barney, was abducted in the early 1960s), her alien visitors decided to share information with her and answer her questions before she was released. Betty noticed maps on a table in the bridge area. Some of the maps were rolled up and others were laid open. Some were clearly aerial maps of earth, while others were of a planet unfamiliar to Betty. Alien symbols identified the land and water masses instead of English symbols, or symbols from any language Betty was aware of globally.

I believe now that the visitors who abducted Betty and Barney Hill were not licensed by any legitimate organization from their world. They were rogue poachers, aka ‘pirates’ who flew under the radar, trying to remain undetected in order to illegally harvest precious DNA from the inhabitants of earth for resale in an interstellar underworld. They operated much like drug cartels do here on earth, and I am sure their profits are just as grossly huge.

This criminal element of alien visitors needed to use old fashioned ways to navigate during poaching abductions on earth in order that they would not be identified through the established and highly advanced GPS technology available to space travelers from their world. Maps insured the safest way for them to remain anonymous. Whilst before I believed Betty Hill had 'made up' the map story in her abduction accounts, I now believe with all my heart that her abductors were forced to use these primitive navigational guides to remain hidden. They operated in the shadows of space.

A decade later, one abductee described a painful operation performed on her by aliens in order to implant a tracking device. When I first read this, I dismissed it immediately. In the advanced technological world of the aliens, or at least the alien visitors I had met, tracking devices were introduced to my system by a simple nasal spray releasing billions of nanoparticles designed as microscopic GPS units. Again, I thought this was a 'made up' story and that the woman had not truly been abducted. Then, I remembered the maps Betty saw, and the reason the alien poachers needed to use them. The same was true when aliens used crude, surgically implanted tracking devices instead of the advanced nasal spray nanoparticles available to licensed visitors. They were not licensed. The nanoparticles used as GPS tracking devices immediately notify appropriate organizations when they become 'active'. The primitive and antique surgically implanted devices would not be picked up by interstellar GPS 'towers'. Again, this woman had been the victim of unauthorized and unlicensed poachers.

At this point I am expecting my readers to be outraged. Aren't all the aliens illegal poachers? If it were possible, I would recommend that my readers ask Alaskan moose and reindeer or African lions and tigers if we are 'legitimate'. We do it because we can, and most of the time we track them for purposes of research that will ultimately better their world and protect their species: most of the time.

‘My Animal Sanctuary’

My Bright Friends, those caring individuals that began visiting me when I was an infant in Tucson, Arizona in 1947 belonged to a legitimate organization from their world whose purpose was to protect and study humans. Some of them were almost human, others were partly human. Both groups conducted the visits according to strict guidelines and standards of ethics and with great concern for the well-being of the lifeform they were studying, namely me.

From my earliest memories of being taken on board an awaiting ship in the desert midnight, I remember one extremely clear action: they always covered my eyes either with their ‘hands’ or a hood. When they used their hands, I would open my eyes and look at the beautiful ship. It was easier to do when the little ones held me, as their ‘hands’ had fewer digits to cover my eyes with.

Although I do not believe I suffer from post-traumatic stress syndrome related to these twenty-five years of visits, I find myself reacting emotionally to documentaries about human caretakers and their relationships to the animals they are studying and protecting in preserves and sanctuaries. At the points in these documentaries when animals are tranquilized or having ‘hoods’ placed over their eyes,

I flash back to being 'hooded' myself during the very early visitations when I was a young child (1-10 years). I do not recall being 'hooded' during later visits, such as during the 'harvesting years' (11-19 years). During this second phase, I was more heavily sedated perhaps because I was older and had attained my full height and also perhaps because the procedures were going to be uncomfortable for me. I still remembered much from this second phase of visits, especially the return journeys. My eyes were not covered, but I was heavily sedated. This sedation lasted for some period after I returned home. A feeling of total body paralysis was common as I lay in my bed. My eyes were open and I wanted to speak out. I could not. I could breathe, but I could not move any other muscles. Someone was close by monitoring me as I came 'out of it'. I could not see them clearly, but I knew this individual was the caring male that had watched over me for many years. He cared deeply about me; it was almost a type of love. I felt the same about him. Once I could move my limbs, I relaxed into a deep, peaceful sleep. I needed this, because the journeys home were frightening to me, no matter how many times they occurred. I felt I was pushed off of a steep cliff into the darkness of space. I would fall at an incredible speed, but I never hit the bottom of the cliff. Even the total paralysis did not scare me as much. My eyes were never covered, however even though they were open I could not see anything but the black space I was 'falling' through. I guess they knew what they were doing, as I always returned in one piece.

Many of the caretakers in the television programs about animal rescues and sanctuaries become emotional when their subjects are returned to their home environments. It was exactly the same with my visitors. They would become extremely emotional and sad to see me go. Even as a young child, I would hold onto them fiercely and beg to remain with them; I loved them so. They explained 'it was not to be'; I needed to return. They watched tears fall from my child eyes, and I watched their 'hearts' cry. My visitors were benevolent and well-intentioned, just as the individuals caring for the animals in the television programs are. I have written about the 'other' type of visitor I was warned about. They are the 'poachers' of their world, just as 'poachers' of our world are brutal and violent to animals: karma.

'Bearing Witness'

Not until I became a grandmother and reached the age of 65 did I realize I had to bear witness to visitations by an advanced, benevolent species not only during the first twenty-five years of my life, but for all my life. Most of the visits, and the clear memories of those visits, happened during those first twenty-five years. This is the time period, 1947-1972, that these essays are based on. However, the conclusions drawn from those experiences are a result of a lifetime of living and observing my own species. Had I not become a mother and grandmother I may never have realized the connection between those visitors and us, even though they had communicated many times over that 'we were family; we were related'. I also realized at my advanced age that if I did not begin to record my experiences, along with information that was transferred to me as a result of these visits, I may run out of time. I strive to remain true to the memories and hope that my recall is not unfairly influenced by my life experiences. Historians throughout time have faced this same struggle. I am not a historian. I am an aged human mother, grandmother and former teacher and these essays are my witness accounts.

We learn about past historical events, important to the evolution and progress of our species, by studying the evidence left us. Sometimes this evidence is buried under centuries of rubble, while other historical clues are documented on tablets and scrolls put in safe harbors such as caves until we 'discover' them. Even odd inclusions in the paintings of past masters offer insight into a recurring and repeating theme through the ages. We have been visited by an advanced group of individuals since our first appearance on the planet earth. The evidence is on cave walls, in beautiful paintings and even documented in the Bible, Torah and other religious texts. The evidence proves one undeniable truth: we are connected to them and they to us. Our actions and continuance as a species are important imperatives to their own survival. Of this, I am convinced.

In order to continue documenting my memories, I ask God for guidance each day. I am a Christian, however I believe that all religions are to be respected and that they are connected in the belief of a creator. I believe there is a God Particle that is an intrinsic part of the universe, the galaxies and solar systems within the universe, the planets and celestial bodies... down to the simplest existing lifeforms. In my own lifetime I have witnessed the legalization of abortions and capital punishment as well as horrific acts of genocide in wartorn regions of the earth. We, humans, are capable of great good and great evil. My visitors not only informed me of our connection to them, but also that there were others in their world that were not well-intentioned in their treatment of us. I believe I know who these others are, as well as some of the selfish, willfull acts of evil they have imposed on many of us. My visitors were benevolent and well-intentioned and it grieved them to make me aware that some individuals in their world were capable of evil. How ironic that in both their world and our world the battle between good and evil seems to infiltrate and define our basic instincts. It is a battle as old as creation itself.

'Amazing and Insidious Future Technology'

This is one of the most difficult subjects I will write about. Religions regard an individual's soul as an ethereal, sacred, entity; an entity only God should deal with. Sadly, the more we progress and conquer barriers with advanced technology, modern humans disregard the human 'soul' with comforting justifications and very little afterthought. Abortions are a common, legal practice in most states. Capital punishment by lethal injection is still a part of the justice system, and assisted suicide is a welcome option for many facing a painful exit by a terminal illness. In our minds the body houses the 'soul', therefore the consideration of the 'soul' is disregarded in our acceptance of these practices in our 'modern' world. It seems impossible to consider new and more egregious technology could be a part of a world future human descendants will live in. As always, laws and restrictions concerning matters of life and death will undoubtedly exist in the future, just as they exist in our world. However, laws and restrictions may not be enough to stop misuse of the amazing technology yet to be discovered by humankind; technology that will test our moral compass to its limits as it blinds, dazzles and gives us powers beyond belief.

During the early years of my visitations (ages

1-10), I was 'abducted' (there is no other word) on a regular basis. First, my body was put in a paralytic state, and then it was transferred by teleportation to a designated area. When I was very young, I was always 'with' someone else during this process. A Bright Friend would appear in my room, immobilize me and together we were teleported to a desert area and an awaiting ship. I vividly remember arriving in the desert with my 'Bright Friend' and seeing the beautiful ship surrounded by brilliant light. During the second part of those first twenty-five years (ages 11-19), I was alone when I was transported to and from my visits. Although someone always remained with me after I was returned from a harvesting procedure, we traveled separately; we were transported individually rather than together. Their advanced technology of teleportation, as well as their ability to manipulate the molecules of solid walls allowing us to 'pass' through them, paled in comparison to an important part of the teleportation process. My body was reduced to the size of nanoparticles for this process. In order for that to happen, my physical DNA was quantified and given a numerical equivalent. They did this to my soul DNA as well. The energy that made up my 'soul' was quantified and issued a numerical equivalent. These numbers were used in the successful transfer of my body and soul to another location. Perhaps the above description of teleportation seems unlikely to my readers. The best analogy I can offer would be someone today trying to explain how a fax machine works to someone alive a century ago: grasping the concept is difficult. Indeed, the concept of a human soul being substantial and tangent enough to quantify might rankle my more religious readers. To this I can only point out that a century ago the subject of immaculate conception was dealt with by clergy only. Today, and I do not mean any disrespect, in vitro fertilization makes conception possible for many couples...immaculately.

My visitors were a licensed, ethical and benevolent group of researchers who treated me like 'precious cargo'. They tried never to frighten me or misuse their abilities with me. However, they also made me aware of 'others' in their world that carried on illegal, and highly profitable, practices using powerful technology, at our expense: the humans they illegally abducted. Beyond even the illegal abductions and poaching of our DNA, ova and sperm, other ill-intentioned beings taunted many individuals by temporarily putting their 'spirits or souls' in another person's body for entertainment purposes. What we identify as paranormal activity, and even possession, many times is the result of just such illegal actions. These activities are outlawed in their world, and if they are found out the punishments are draconian. Perhaps some of the lesser egregious activities, like a poltergeist or friendly ghost, might even be 'legal' in their world. Possession is not legal, and I can't imagine a future that would sanction it.

Medical professionals in their future world will use this technology to help patients. However, permission to use this technology will be given only after a thorough investigative process of both the patient and the doctor(s) involved. One can only imagine the possibilities open to an enterprising black-market entertainment 'mogul'. Similarities between my experiences and the experiences of the many individuals who have been 'haunted' are too many to disregard. They feel paralyzed, they see individuals walking through walls and many feel a sensation of being possessed. I never felt 'possessed', however I was routinely paralyzed and I not only saw individuals walk 'through' walls, I did it as well (with their help). Just as we watch reality television, individuals in their future world must find our reactions to these 'paranormal' experiences delightfully entertaining. A century ago, the first silent movies gave society the opportunity to voyeuristically 'experience' what the actors on the screen experienced. In future centuries, more advanced and intrusive types of 'voyeurism' will be possible, though not legal. It will be produced and sold by unethical, greedy individuals who will risk being caught because of the huge profits involved.

Out of fairness, in future times technology and

medical advances will redefine 'death' as we know it, just as our technology and medical advances have redefined life and death for us when compared to practices centuries past. If 'death' and the 'soul' are redefined, a different level of criminal will be involved: a more 'legitimate' criminal, the most dangerous type. And although polite society might outwardly frown upon this practice, they might secretly delight in it and support it, just as drinking alcohol was a common practice among the gentry during prohibition. As my Bright Friends communicated to me: 'we are related; we are family', and it seems the more things change, the more they stay the same.

When I was a child, growing up in Tucson, Arizona, some of my friends were of Native American origin. They wouldn't allow their pictures to be taken by school photographers. When I asked them 'why?', they told me the photograph would capture and imprison their soul. I can think of no better analogy to conclude this essay about life, death and our souls. Perhaps another way to measure progress is in the redefinition of life processes. Will religious beliefs be tested? They always are. In the century just past, abortions and capital punishment began religious debates that continue today.

Final Thoughts

In 1595 Zacharias Janseen and his father Hans, both glassmakers, invented an early form of the microscope. They were not alone. Other inventors would follow, each improving the instrument that would help take superstition out of medical diagnoses for many ailments. Before bacteria could be seen under the scrutinizing lens of the microscope, everything from headaches to sudden unexplained ailments resulting in death could be blamed on negative spiritual forces, or curses. Today, four hundred years later, we can identify bacteria as the culprit in many deaths. However, my grandmother Kalliopi believed that some ailments were caused by people being targeted by the 'evil eye', a belief alive and well in many parts of the present world. I personally believe that even cancer is aggravated by a person's spiritual negative energy. I have no doubt that just as the microscope could 'prove' that bacteria was responsible for many illnesses and not curses, in future years the 'soul' will be quantified as existing independent of the body after the death of the body. Its disposition will be in question; perhaps dependent on the positive or negative spiritual energy of the person. And that is the very definition of religion...I believe.

Information regarding the 'energy' of the soul, or

even the definition of the 'soul', is sparse. Because of the wedded interaction between the brain and soul in living humans, I (respectfully) would like to use a computer analogy for illustration. We can define computers as electronic or mechanical brains. Any interaction on a computer is recorded on a hard drive. Even if the information is deleted or destroyed, and even if the computer is dismantled, the information remains on the hard drive. Assuming the actual hard drive of a particular computer is destroyed, the information exists in cyberspace. Once information is created by the computer, it is impossible to destroy it. I am taking a huge leap here, but I believe this is the closest analogy to the existence of a human soul that I can find. We are born with a blank or pure soul; our life existence defines this until the day we die (or until the day our bodies stop living). I am convinced that our soul continues on in a form of cohesive energy for some time after our body stops living. With time, that energy will be reabsorbed into other living entities. Whether this energy is reabsorbed as a whole or in many smaller increments is determined by many factors. The factors may be as basic as where and how a person died or how young/old the person was. I am convinced that someday a mathematical equivalent will be created for a person's soul; each soul will have a distinctive equivalent. It is too late in my life for me to study mathematics to the point where I could prove this. I hope I am still alive to witness this become a reality, along with an official worldwide acknowledgement of UFOs and alien visitors. Time will tell.

The Final Harbour

From wave-kissed shores
They mapped on sand
Unmoored their boats
And pushed off land

They looked toward heaven
To guide their ships
They looked toward heaven
And asked 'what if?'

In silver ships
They sailed past stars
Past Venus, Saturn
Earth and Mars

Through galaxies of time and space
They quested past each wondrous place

They soared and sailed
And quested farther
Oh, when and where
The final harbour

(written specifically for this book, "Bright Friends: The First Twenty-Five Years of Visitations 1947-1972" by Karen Kalliopi Papagapitos 2016)

About the Author

Karen Kalliopi Papagapitos earned a degree in Education from the University of Arizona and taught the children of migrant farm workers near the border town of Nogales, Arizona. She is a Fellow of the World Literary Academy as well as a member of The Academy of American Poets. Karen is the author of three other books. She currently lives in the Bronx, New York.

Printed in the United States
By Bookmasters